LIFE
in
CHRIST

Other Abingdon Press Books by Steve Harper

Holy Love: A Biblical Theology for Human Sexuality
Five Marks of a Methodist: The Fruit of a Living Faith
Stepping Aside, Moving Ahead
For the Sake of the Bride

Steve Harper

LIFE in CHRIST

The Core of Intentional Spirituality

Abingdon Press™
Nashville

LIFE IN CHRIST:
THE CORE OF INTENTIONAL SPIRITUALITY

Copyright © 2020 by Abingdon Press

Library of Congress Control Number: 2020937635
ISBN: 978-1-7910-0470-5

20 21 22 23 24 25 26 27 28 29—10 9 8 7 6 5 4 3 2 1
MANUFACTURED IN THE UNITED STATES OF AMERICA

Dedications

To Jeannie,
my true love and soul mate on the journey of life in Christ for fifty years!

To John and Allison, Katrina and Chris,
our beloved children and their spouses.

To Zoe, Isaac, and James,
delightful grandchildren.

And to my students,
who made decades of teaching a joy.

"Our full spiritual life is life in wisdom, life in Christ."
—*Thomas Merton,* New Seeds of Contemplation

Contents

Contents

Preface

I have been thinking about this book for over twenty years. In fact, I have attempted to write it several times. Each time, however, before I got far, something inside me said, "It's not time. You're not ready. You must live further into the things you want to write about." Well, here I am at seventy-two years of age. I am continuing to live into everything you are about to read. I have not arrived, but a sense of timeliness has emerged and I am doing my best to honor that inner conviction.

My sense of timeliness is larger than the fact that I am an older adult, larger even than my personal thoughts about the ideas in this book. This sense that I have is a conviction that we are at a pivotal moment in history, a moment when the decisions we make will shape the future, and will do so probably much faster than we think. Sister Joan Chittister said it simply: "The time is now."[1] I agree, and that belief has given rise to my writing. This book is intentionally prophetic; that is, it is a call

---

1. Joan Chittister, *The Time is Now* (Convergent Books, 2019).

to live as God intends us to live amid a world that too often works against our doing so.

When I first thought about this book years ago, one of the motivating statements came from E. Stanley Jones in the introduction to his book, *Mastery*: "Modern man knows everything about life except how to live it. . . . We are enlightened, but I question whether we are more enlivened."[2] His words sunk into me deeply when I first read them and they remain influential for my writing now. Indeed, we are enlightened. From the time Jones wrote these words in 1955 until now, that enlightenment has increased exponentially. Since I first read his words in the early 1990s to today, the human race has achieved breathtaking accomplishments. There is no sign that that is going to stop.

Jones's question, however, is now my question: We are enlightened, but are we enlivened? In some ways, the answer is surely, "Yes." Human life is magnificent and we Christians are not dualists. We do not separate the material and immaterial, body and soul. We find joy in many of the same things in which everyone else finds joy. In other ways, however, the answer is still "No." Almost every day, the media shows us, in stark detail, how far we have to go. Woven into this realization, as Jones genuinely saw it, is the profound hunger for life that has been with us from the very beginning of creation. We long to be enlivened. We all do. That's why I am writing this book, right now.

The essential message I want to communicate is in the text, as it is in all books, but I want to emphasize that I have included numerous references to other books, especially those by

---

2. E. Stanley Jones, *Mastery* (Pierce & Washabaugh, 1955), v.

E. Stanley Jones.[3] We receive light from many lamps as we live our lives. I hope you enjoy reading this book and benefit from it. Do pay attention to the references and the reading lists, and use them to further your exploration of abundant living. God has bespangled life in Christ all over the place!

Steve Harper

---

3. My references to E. Stanley Jones are intentional. I consider him the overall most influential spiritual guide in my life, theologically and experientially. I hope you will become familiar with his writings if you have not already done so. Happily, Abingdon Press has reprinted many of his books, with others still to come.

Introduction

Nicodemus came to Jesus because he was hungering for something more. His life as a religious person and spiritual leader was genuine, but not complete. He was open to further light. He was yearning for it. He believed Jesus had come from God (John 3:2) and, as such, that Jesus might have something to share with him that could enrich his life beyond his current experience. He came to Jesus at night, probably to avoid calling attention to his visit. Jesus welcomed Nicodemus and entered into a conversation with him that was simultaneously mysterious and magnetic.

In many ways, Nicodemus's story is the story of us all. He is a stand-in for anyone who, as Barbara Brown Taylor describes them,

> know[s] there is more to life than what meets the eye. They have drawn close to this 'More' in nature, in love, in art, in grief. They would be happy for someone to teach them how to spend more time in the presence of this deeper reality, but when they visit the places where such knowledge is supposed to be found, they often find the rituals hollow and the language antique. Even religious people are vulnerable to this longing.[1]

1. Barbara Brown Taylor, *An Altar in the World* (HarperCollins, 2009), loc 73.

Make no mistake. Nicodemus was one of the religious people. In fact, he was an esteemed religious leader. But as Barbara Brown Taylor wrote above, Nicodemus was not exempt from a spiritual longing that urged him to move beyond his current experience. Like him, we don't go far in life without realizing that our lives are incomplete. Much of the time, we cannot put into words what we mean by incompleteness; it is more of an unspoken intuition than it is a clearly identified reality. It is a sense that there is a difference between being alive and living. Everyone is alive, but not everyone is living—at least not fully. So quite naturally, we go in search of more life and find, as we do (as Nicodemus did), that there is more than being born of the flesh; there is something about being born of the Spirit (John 3:6). Again, like Nicodemus, it is a view of life that simultaneously bothers us and draws us in.

The hunger for something more is universal and timeless. It has revealed itself in philosophies and theologies written over the ages. But it shows up more simply in everyday ways. Years ago, in the popular song, "I Gotta Be Me," Sammy Davis Jr. sang about looking for more out of life:

And I won't give up this dream
Of life that keeps me alive.[2]

The phrase "this dream of life that keeps me alive" describes our quest to live more fully than we are currently living. The challenge for us, as it was for Nicodemus, is to discern what will provide us with abundant life. We are weary of being handed life substitutes that diminish us rather than enrich us.

2. "I Gotta Be Me" was written by Walter Marks in 1968 and first appeared in the Broadway musical *Golden Rainbow*.

In the Christian tradition we often call this quest spiritual formation—that is, being "born of the Spirit" in ways that take us beyond where we are and move us into what the Bible calls "the new creation" (2 Cor 5:17)—what Jesus called "abundant living" (John 10:10, author's translation). The summary phrase for this is "life in Christ," and in scripture there is no better place to explore it than in Paul's letter to the Galatians. This book emerges from his letter, both because it is a firsthand account of Paul's experience of abundant living, and also because he wrote it to help others discern between genuine life and life substitutes. He wrote it to help people become new creations (Gal 6:15). I hope to write about that too, and to do it in a way that will be helpful to you.

But let me be clear: I am not writing as one who has arrived, but only as a companion on the way that leads to life, life in Christ. I have been on the path for more than fifty years, and still the journey unfolds. There is still far more mystery than fact. Indeed, it cannot be any other way because God is infinite; life with God is never-ending. That's why Nicodemus found Jesus's description of it to be both awesome and attractive. It's why I continue to be drawn into the spiritual life. If you are reading this as one on the journey, you know what I mean.

If you are newer to the journey, I hope you will receive this book as an invitation—an invitation for you to look at your life perhaps in ways you have never done before. I hope you will read it as a conversation between you and me—two fellow travelers on the path. There's something of Nicodemus in all of us.

Using This Book

To assist you in reading this book, I have provided a reflection guide that you can use, either personally or in a group setting (appendix one). In addition to reading this book individually, I hope you will also use it with others. We grow best in conversation and community. At the end of the book, I have written a brief small-group guide to assist you as you do this (appendix two). The guide can be used as you work through the book together, and it can be a model for any small-group meeting. This guide also offers additional ways I hope this book will be a springboard for additional formation.

First, I have provided numerous footnotes. If a particular subject attracts your attention, you can follow it to go beyond what I have written. The footnotes reveal the sources that have formed my life in Christ, and they can be doorways into further discoveries about your spiritual formation. I once heard an author say, "If you really want to know who I am and how I got to be this way, look at the footnotes." I agree. The footnotes may be more valuable than what I have written because they will take you into the worlds and words of others.

Second, I have linked aspects of this book to the writings of E. Stanley Jones (appendix three). You'll find many references to him in the footnotes. Not only do I consider him the main mentor (theologically and spiritually) in my faith, but also I believe his insights are much needed today. Happily, Abingdon Press has reprinted many of his books. I have also provided an "E. Stanley Jones Reading List" at the end of the book, so that you can let him guide you into a deeper and wider life in Christ.

Third, the themes in this book span Christian history. In appendix four I have provided a list of devotional classics that you can use to trace many of this book's themes (and others too) across the centuries. As the writer of Hebrews wrote, we are surrounded by a great cloud of witnesses. This list can introduce you to some of the women and men who have lived "in Christ" before us.

Fourth, there are additional books that I want you to know about. Another list in the appendices suggests other authors besides what I have put into the footnotes. This list further expands what you can read (appendix five). There are also some excellent one-volume reference books that can open the door to a deep-and-wide exploration of the spiritual life; I have listed some of them in appendix six.

Finally, I hope this book will become part of a sustained ministry of spiritual formation in your local church. Appendix seven connects you with spiritual formation ministries, which you can use to forge those connections.

Chapter One
The Vision

I t's been more than fifty years, but I still cannot watch a video of Martin Luther King Jr. delivering his "I Have a Dream" speech without being moved once again. If I watch it at just the right time, the video brings tears and other emotions, just as it did when I first watched King's speech live. One writer described King's speech this way: "The nation stood on the brink of racial civil war. It needed a prophet who could help see through the smoke left by gunpowder and bombs."[1] King's speech moved many of us and it continues to do so, precisely because it cast a vision for life beyond what so many were (and are) experiencing.

We live in relation to our visions; our visions of God, of others, and of ourselves shape our attitudes and actions. The writer of Proverbs understood this, writing, "Where there's no vision, the people get out of control" (29:18). Without vision, there is no center of meaning around which a circumference of activities is formed. Without vision, there is no core substance to give shape to our lives. Paul found this to be true in Galatia. The vision

---

1. James Melvin Washington, ed., *I Have a Dream: Writings and Speeches that Changed the World* (HarperOne, 1992), 101.

that he had cast with the new Christians when he was with them had been lost, not as a result of gunpowder and bombs, but because others had come into the community after he had left and tried to substitute "another gospel" for the real one (Gal 1:6). Paul wrote back to his friends, recasting the vision for life, which some had already deserted for life substitutes. As we will see, Paul was calling the Galatians back to grace and away from legalism, a return he described as ceasing to live in the flesh and living in the Spirit instead. It is a vision we need in our own day. We are always tempted to find life through rules rather than relationships, through dogmas rather than God.

Paul summarized this vision in Galatians 2:20: "I have been crucified with Christ and I no longer live, but Christ lives in me." He cast a vision for life—abundant life—in Christ. The original Greek reads: "I no longer live as an I, but Christ lives in me." Paul was saying that when we live in Christ, we no longer live as people driven by ego, but as people defined by imago (Gen 1:26-28). But what kind of life is this? It is life described in Greek as *zoe.*

Returning to Nicodemus's conversation with Jesus in John 3, it is the difference between living in the flesh and living in the Spirit—the same difference Paul unpacks in his letter to the Galatians. The Greeks understood life in two dimensions: *bios* and *zoe. Bios* means *physical life* and its meaning includes everything that makes up the regular course of our lives, what we would call "life in general."[2] It is important for us to recognize that there is much good found in this life. In and of itself, it is not bad or evil. It includes a host of blessings and benefits and it bestows a wealth of talents and capacities. But *bios* is simply not the full definition

---

2. William D. Mounce, *Complete Expository Dictionary of Old and New Testament Words* (Zondervan, 2006), 404–405.

of *life*. It is only when *bios* is misunderstood as the sum of life that the concept of *bios* becomes a life-diminisher rather than a life-giver. To put it simply, *bios* belongs on the circumference, not at the center. When egotism or ethnocentrism puts *bios* at the center, life goes off the rails.[3]

In Galatia, the new Christians were reverting to thinking in terms of *bios* and they were doing it in a particular way. They were removing God's grace and replacing it with human effort (Gal 3:3). They were doing it by reverting to legalism, to living according to the law, which ultimately meant putting themselves at the center of existence, living a performance-oriented life (which enabled them to measure their righteousness and judge the righteousness of others) rather than putting God (the Spirit) at the center and living a faith-oriented life that looked to Christ as the life-giver. The Galatian error is the abiding error that prevents us from living abundantly. It is the error of starting with ourselves rather than with God, living a "life in the flesh" (*bios*) instead of a "life in the Spirit" (*zoe*). This error views means as ends, ascribing ultimate value to lesser things. Once Paul learned that this was happening in Galatia, he immediately confronted the error and restored the vision of abundant living—of life that is given substance and shape by Christ. Jesus had made it clear: "I am...the life" (John 14:6). Now, as the risen Christ, he is the *zoe*.

We do not live in a *zoe*-shaped world. Richard Foster has described the contemporary error, noting that "Michael Gerson has observed that our culture is constantly shouting to us, 'Blessed are the proud. Blessed are the ruthless. Blessed are the

---

3. I will use egotism/ethnocentrism to describe the essence of the original sin in its individual and collective expressions. This is what Thomas Merton and others called "the false self." We will explore this in more detail farther along in the book.

shameless. Blessed are those who hunger and thirst after fame.' This all-pervasive dysfunction in our culture today makes it nearly impossible for us to have a clear vision of spiritual progress under God."[4] The first task of a vision for the spiritual life is to confront life substitutes, and doing so in a way that awakens us to awe (the mystery of the spiritual life) and to surrender (the magnetism of the spiritual life), which is the very experience Jesus described in his conversation with Nicodemus.[5] A vision of the spiritual life is immediately and radically prophetic. It calls out falsehood, names what is good, and declares with confidence that God is at work in us to move us away from the one and into the other. It is, as Jesus described it to Nicodemus in John 3, nothing less than a new birth, a birth "from above," a life "born of the Spirit" (3:3, 6 NRSV). Christ is the essence of this life (John 14:6). We see this in a variety of ways.

Life by Christ. Before John had barely begun his gospel, he wrote: "Everything came into being through the Word, and without the Word nothing came into being" (John 1:3). Paul repeated the same thing in his letter to the Colossians: "all things were created by him: both in the heavens and on the earth, the things that are visible and the things that are invisible, whether they are thrones or powers, rulers or authorities, all things were created through him and for him" (Col 1:16). These New Testament passages reflect the wisdom tradition in Judaism, which saw Lady Wisdom beside God (John 1:1 says "with God") creating all things as a master craftsperson (Prov 8:30).

---

4. Richard Foster, *Casting a Vision* (Renovare, 2019), 2.

5. Richard Rohr, *Just This* (CAC Publishing, 2017). Rohr organizes his book around the dimensions of awe and surrender, the two movements being lifted up in our movement into abundant living.

At first glance, this may seem to be abstract theology, but it is far from it. For, what the Bible teaches us is that the sum total of creation—everything, everywhere—is alive by Christ. E. Stanley Jones emphasized this in many of his books, looking at Christ not only as a pervasive presence in all things, but also as the penetration into all things, "written into the nature of reality, written into our blood, nerves tissues, relationships—into everything."[6] As I write these words, and as you read them, we do so as Christ-made people. We did not make ourselves. We are not self-generating.[7] Then, moving beyond our individual lives, the same Christ-made reality extends to the entire cosmos.[8] From the smallest particle to the farthest star, Christ is the maker. We live by Christ.

It is important for us to see this, not as a one-time creation event of the cosmos or of us. It is an ongoing reality. Not only are we not self-originating, we are not self-sustaining. We live by Christ right now. "In God we live, move, and exist" (Acts 17:28). This is one reason why we cannot separate *bios* and *zoe*. Christ has made us with biological and social systems that keep us alive. We do not have to try to stay alive; we are simply alive. Theologically, this means we are not self-sustaining. Jesus described it by saying that we cannot add a moment to our lives (Luke 18:25). Life is by Christ.

Life to Christ. This phrase simply means that we live as God intends when we live in response to the movements of the Spirit in our lives. Jesus described it as following him (Mark 1:17). Paul

---

6. E. Stanley Jones, *The Way* (Abingdon Press, 1946), 7.

7. Dennis Kinlaw, *We Live as Christ* (Francis Asbury Press, 2001), 56–58.

8. I am grateful to Ilia Delio for giving language to the pervasiveness of Christ and often doing so through the insights of Pierre Teilhard de Chardin. Her book, *The Emergent Christ* (Orbis Books, 2011), is a good place to begin to see Christ's universality. Richard Rohr's book, *The Universal Christ* (Convergent Books, 2019), is another must-read on the subject.

referred to it as offering ourselves to God as living sacrifices (Rom 12:1). Life to Christ is summed up in the word *consecration*. We call it *obedience*, a word that means paying attention with the intention of putting into practice what we hear. Life to Christ is attentiveness enacted.[9]

When I was in high school, physical education classes were mandatory. Every afternoon, Coach Middleton would lead us in reflex drills. He would stand in front of us and make some kind of movement (e.g., turning to the side while running in place), and we were supposed to do the same thing as quickly as we could. We kept our eyes on him and did whatever he did. In many ways this is the spiritual life—paying attention to Christ and doing what he does as quickly as we can. We are not self-referent; we are God-directed. We become so primarily through reading scripture and responding to what we read. We consecrate our lives by being attentive to Christ, to what Brother Lawrence called the practice of the presence of God.[10] It is a practice that exemplifies ordinary holiness and fidelity to God in little things. In fact, Brother Lawrence wrote that he came to see removing a stick out of the road so a traveler would not trip over it was as holy an act of devotion as receiving the Holy Sacrament. That's quite a statement, but it is true. We live to Christ; that is, we aim to honor and glorify him in all that we think, say, and do.

Life with Christ. After Jesus called the twelve apostles, the first thing he asked was for them to be with him (Mark 3:14). They

9. Michael Mayne develops this idea in his book, *Giving Attention: Becoming What You Truly Are* (Canterbury Press, 2018).

10. Brother Lawrence's book, *The Practice of the Presence of God*, was written in the seventeenth century and is a devotional classic, a mainstay in understanding what it means to pay attention to God and to put into practice what we hear in every moment and detail of our lives. This book is available in a multitude of editions and formats.

could do this literally; we must do it figuratively—but no less genuinely. To be "with Christ" is to be in communion with him through prayer. It is to be with him in desire (e.g., Matt 6:10 KJV, "Thy kingdom come. Thy will be done in earth, as it is in heaven"). It is to follow him as he leads us from one aspect of life to another (Mark 1:17).

To live with Christ is another way of reiterating that he is the center. He gathered a diverse group of followers and they lived in relation to him. To live with Christ is also to live in community. When we live with Christ, we live with each other because Christ is our life, individually and collectively. Moreover, when we live with Christ, we do so continuously. As William Barclay put it, "Others might come and go; the crowd might be there one day and away the next; others might be fluctuating and spasmodic in their attachment to Jesus, but these twelve were to identify their lives with his life; they were to live with him all the time."[11] All of this is a way of saying that when we consecrate our lives to Christ, we enter into a 24/7 life of consecration, not a consecration that is limited to certain days of the week or a consecration that applies only to the "religious" aspects of our lives.

There is more, however: to be with Christ is to be recipients of all that he has to give us. His final promise is our ultimate confidence: "I myself will be with you every day until the end of the present age" (Matt 28:20). Jesus never asks anything of us that he is not willing to give to us! When we speak of life with Christ, we are also saying that he is with us. That is, we are in a genuine relationship—one of mutuality and reciprocity.

11. William Barclay, *The Daily Study Bible: The Gospel of Mark* (Westminster Press, 1957), 69–70.

Robert Boyd Munger wrote of this in his devotional classic, *My Heart, Christ's Home*. In addition to all the reasons we can think of for why we need to be with Christ, Munger adds the fact that Christ needs to be with us, having him simply say, "You have been thinking of the quiet time, of Bible study and prayer, as a means for your own spiritual growth. This is true, but you have forgotten that this means something to me also. Remember, I love you....Remember I want to be with you!"[12] To live with Christ is to live in a give-and-take relationship—with Christ, and with everyone and everything else!

Life in Christ. As with any other relationship, the more time we spend with someone or something, the farther we live into the reality of the relationship. In the 24/7 life with Christ, we move farther into abundant life. We live in Christ (Phil 1:21) and Christ lives in us (Gal 2:2). The phrase "in Christ" is used 172 times in the New Testament, and it is the quality of life Jesus said he came to give us. E. Stanley Jones described it this way: "The phrase 'in Christ' is the ultimate phrase in the Christian faith, for it locates us in a Person—the Divine Person—and it locates us in Him here and now."[13]

The enrichment of our relationship with Christ is contained in the word often translated as *abide*, and in more-modern translations as *remain*. I have preferred *abide* for a long time, but I have now come to see that the word *remain* gets even more to the heart

---

12. Robert Boyd Munger, *My Heart—Christ's Home*, rev. ed. (InterVarsity Press, 1986), 15–16. Originally published in 1954, this little book remains a gem in spiritual formation literature. Munger considers the heart and names aspects of the heart similarly to rooms in a house. Christ enters the heart and, little by little, transforms everything.

13. E. Stanley Jones, *In Christ* (Abingdon Press, 1961), 14. I know of no finer exploration of life in Christ than the one Jones provided, and he did so in a book that can be used in one's daily devotional time.

of the matter (John 15:4, et al). We noted above that life with Christ is a continuous reality, so to live this way is to remain in him—and he in us. In this remaining, there is both a deepening and a broadening of our relationship with Christ and our life in him. It takes both breadth and depth for our lives to mature as God intends. Depth without breadth eventually becomes narrowness. Breadth without depth turns into superficiality. It is when depth and breadth grow together that we grow in the grace and knowledge of our Lord Jesus Christ (2 Pet 3:18).

Life like Christ. When people are in relationships with each other for a long time, they naturally share things in common; this happens in friendships, but especially in marriages. We become like those with whom we relate. The same thing happens as our relationship with Christ becomes more continuous and extended. Paul called it having the mind of Christ (Phil 2:5), having the attitude and disposition of Jesus. The usual name for it is *Christlikeness.*[14]

Taking the Christian tradition as a whole, the highest thing we can say about people is that they are Christlike. Life in Christ centers us in him, and Christ-centeredness produces Christlike character.[15] In Galatians, *Christlikeness* is summed up and described as the fruits of the Spirit: love, joy, peace, patience, kindness, goodness, faithfulness, gentleness, and self-control (Gal 5:22-23). Life like Christ begins in the heart (inwardly) and expresses itself in our behavior (outwardly). Life like Christ defines

---

14. Because our relationship with Christ is with the risen, excarnate Christ (not the incarnate Christ), the life described in this chapter is through the presence of the Spirit in our lives. Even though we use the word *Christlikeness* in this section of the chapter, we can never be like the universal Christ, the second person of the Holy Trinity. Christlikeness is described relative to Jesus, the Word made flesh. We can be like him in that respect because he became like us in the incarnation.

15. Jones, *In Christ*, 373 (Week 51, Saturday).

both our characters and our conduct. Saint Francis described it in a prayer: "Lord, make me an instrument of your peace." It is a making of us by the Spirit, which then becomes a manifestation of the Spirit through us as instruments of God's peace. We will look more closely at Christlikeness in chapter five.

Life for Christ. In *life for Christ*, we have come to the place that St. Francis describes in his prayer, that of being instruments. Jesus put it this way: "As the Father sent me, so I am sending you" (John 20:21). We are "sent ones"—that is, people meant to live in the world as representatives and reflections of Christ. We have many jobs, but one vocation (one calling): to live for Christ in whatever we do and wherever we go. We are apostles.

This final phrase in the description of abundant living eliminates once and for all the idea that our lives do not matter; quite the contrary, our lives matter more than we could ever imagine! In fact, the word *Christian* means a "Christ one" or a "little Christ." The life we have explored in this chapter is one of radical (essential) oneness with Christ, and out of that oneness we live in whatever places and ways that constitute our daily life. This is the essence of holiness: doing the next thing we have to do and doing it for Jesus.[16] We live for Christ.

In this chapter we have cast the vision for the spiritual life by looking at six dimensions of it in relation to Christ. By doing so, it is clear why Paul said, "For to me, living is Christ" (Phil 1:21 NRSV), and why he made such living the hallmark of his definition of life in his letter to the Galatians. Before we conclude this chapter, we must not fail to note that we are describing a life that

---

16. This idea is at the heart of classical Christian spirituality, and is described in detail in Jean-Pierre de Caussade's book, *Abandonment to Divine Providence*, which is a compilation of a series of retreat talks he gave in the seventeenth century about holy living. The book remains in print, in both e-book and traditional formats.

unfolds, not one that happens all at once or is fully contained in any single experience. Telling Nicodemus that he needed a "new birth" was Jesus's way of saying the same thing, for a birth is only the beginning of a larger and longer life.[17]

Christ is our life (Col 3:4). But we are, to use E. Stanley Jones's words, only Christians "in the making."[18] How can it be otherwise, when we are dealing with an infinite God? We never "arrive"; we are always "on the way," following the one who is the way. No matter where we are in the spiritual life, we can always take another step into faith; the Spirit is at work in us, and is motivating us to do so. The vision of the spiritual life is not one of attainment, but one of alignment—not with an idea, but with a person, who is Jesus Christ our lord. The rest of this book is an enlargement of this theme.

---

17. Sadly, we have misconstrued the idea of "new birth" as a testimony of attainment rather than as a trajectory of advancement. Jesus could not have been clearer about the unfolding of abundant life than by referring to it as a birth; we are the ones who have come to ascribe a finality to the idea.

18. E. Stanley Jones, *A Song of Ascents* (Abingdon Press, 1968), 19.

Chapter Two
The Movement

When I was a child, my dad measured my height. I would stand as tall as I could beside the door next to my bedroom. Dad used his fingernail to make an indentation into the wood and I would then move away and look at the mark he had just made. Sure enough, it was always a little higher than the last one. Even though I could not feel it, I was growing; the way I recognized my growth most was having to wear larger clothing. I moved out of one size into a larger one.

Scientists tell us that everything in the cosmos is in motion, from the smallest particle to the farthest star. Nothing is standing still. To be alive is to be in motion. Scientists, however, also tell us that this motion is not so much self-generated as it is responsive to forces beyond the elements themselves. Although much of this remains unknown, we recognize that the universe is in motion because a larger energy activates it; there is some great attraction that propels everything toward expansion.[1]

---

1. Numerous scientific articles confirm this; a specific reference is on the BBC Science Focus website in an article by Dr. Alastair Gunn entitled, "Why is Everything in Motion?" The article is undated; Gunn is a Fellow of the Royal Astronomical Society. https://www.sciencefocus.com/space/why-is-everything-in-motion/.

It should not surprise us, then, that the same reality holds true for our spiritual life. The one who has made all things (John 1:3), has made them with a synchronicity among both visible and invisible things (Rom 1:20, Heb 11:3). Our soul is in motion, and the Bible calls such motion moving from one degree of glory to another (2 Cor 3:18). We are meant to glorify God increasingly and that purpose keeps us in motion. In matters of faith, God is the great attractor, always inviting us into living a wider and deeper life. The type of growth we explore in this book is not the result of compulsion or demand, but rather the effect of the Spirit working in us by love. We are made to grow.

In the largest scheme of things, growth is always "from" something, "to" something. Every movement is a from/to experience. We are always moving from one thing to another. We cannot move toward something without also moving away from something else. In fact, the two movements occur simultaneously; they are two parts of one larger whole. In Christian spirituality, the often-used metaphors for this are those of a journey or a pathway. We will look at these metaphors more closely later in this chapter. For now, we simply want to see that, in every way, we are meant to be moving. Spiritual life is life in motion.

There is no better place in scripture to explore this than Paul's letter to the Galatians. The biblical metaphor for it is moving **from** living in the flesh **to** living in the Spirit (Gal 3:3). The Galatians were moving both ways, and Paul's letter is a focal point for understanding the deformative and formative movements in the spiritual life. We do this by exploring the two words Paul used in his letter: *flesh* (*sarx*) and *spirit* (*pneuma*).

Living in the flesh is deformative, and it diminishes the spiritual life. In using the word *sarx*, however, Paul has more in mind than our literal flesh. *Sarx* describes something more than physicality. If we do not see this, then we risk becoming dualists—people who caricature the flesh as evil and the spirit as good.[2] Paul does not do this, and neither does genuine Christianity. More to the point, *sarx* is what we would typically call *human nature*.[3] When we recognize this, we understand that the flesh/Spirit pairing is not synonymous with the evil/good distinction. Rather, much is commendable about human nature.

E. Stanley Jones captured the Christian view this way: "Not that the self in itself is evil, but it is evil if the self becomes the center of itself, becomes God."[4] Paul understands *sarx* to be a problem when it means trying to become righteous through human effort (see Gal 3:3). The flesh is a problem when it falls prey to egotism, a condition that makes us self-centered rather than God-centered, self-righteous rather than being made righteous by grace. Jones again gets to the heart of it when he writes: "Your self on your own hands is a problem and a pain; your self in the hands of God is a possibility and a power."[5] Simply put, selfishness is antithetical to the spiritual life. We must move away from such selfishness.

Paul did not stop after providing a diagnosis. He then moved on to describing the cure: living in the Spirit. Doubtless, he was referring to life that moves in relationship with and in response to the Holy Spirit. This is the Christlikeness we looked at in the

2. To learn more about flesh/spirit, bad/good dualism study Gnosticism. Preceding Christianity, Gnosticism eventually contaminated portions of early Christianity and is likely the philosophical concept Paul was contending with in Galatia.

3. William D. Mounce, *Complete Expository Dictionary of Old and New Testament Words* (Zondervan, 2006), 259.

4. E. Stanley Jones, *Growing Spiritually* (Pierce & Washabaugh, 1953), 15 (Week 3, Sunday). Pagination aligns with the Abingdon Press edition, 1978.

5. Jones, *Growing Spiritually*, 21 (Week 3, Saturday).

last chapter. The Christian spiritual life is a life "of the Spirit." But just as the word *sarx* means more than simply the body, the word *pneuma* also means more than the third person of the Trinity. Spirit is a word that also describes our essence because we are made in God's image.

Living spiritually is not contingent on the Holy Spirit, as much as it is contingent on the human spirit. That is, living spiritually is contingent on whether we are in opposition to the Spirit working in us or whether we are in cooperation with the Spirit's work. Paul's understanding of the Galatians' problem is that they were reverting to living in the flesh, which was clearly an act of the will on their part. From this we learn the amazing and sobering truth that the spiritual life rises and falls within us not in relation to grace (which is constant and abundant) but in relation to the choices we make in response to grace. Very simply, the Galatians lived in the flesh by saying "No" to God; they lived in the Spirit by saying "Yes" to God.

Paul's letter to the Galatians is revealing with respect to the place of the will in spiritual formation. There are no formulas in the spiritual life, but there is a principle that describes the spiritual life: grace + response = growth. This is living in the Spirit. Living in the flesh operates by a principle as well: grace + resistance = decline. For Paul, the Galatians; resistance was their choice to revert from living in response to grace to living in obedience to the law. Paul goes into detail about this in chapters three and four of Galatians. We must look at what he wrote back then because it is a message for us now.

We begin by noting that Paul does not say that the law is evil; the law is not against God's promises (Gal 3:21). In fact, the law was given by God, and it reveals covenant living, summed up in the two great commandments: love God (Deut 6:5) and love our neighbor as ourselves (Lev 19:8). The fact that the law is rooted in love means that it is life-oriented, not sin-oriented. So, what's the problem? Why is living by the law what Paul means in Galatians by living in the flesh? Paul answers the question himself: living in the flesh (living by the law) is trying to derive life from something that cannot give life (Gal 3:21). The law's purpose is simultaneously to show what the life of love looks like (both in terms of obedience and disobedience) and to clarify that it is impossible to "keep the Law" through human effort (Gal 2:17, 3:3 JBP). The law is intended to generate humility in us, not hubris. It is meant to bring us to Christ which is to create utter reliance upon grace by the presence and work of the Spirit in and through us (Gal 3:24).

Paul had ministered in Galatia in ways that brought the people to repentance (i.e., looking at life in a new way—the way of grace) and into life in the Spirit. Under the influence of the Judaisers (the legalists), however, they had "fallen away from grace" (Gal 5:4) by reverting to a misunderstanding and misuse of the law. That is, thinking the law is life, when in fact, only Christ is life (John 14:6, Col 3:4). Legalism's problem is that it caters to the ego, encouraging us to put ourselves at the center rather than God. The law does this by creating a performance-oriented faith that can be defined by rules and regulations, and a faith that is measured by our obedience to such rules and regulations. Such an orientation puts us "in charge" and inevitably makes us judgmental because we use the rules and regulations to determine who is "in" and who is "out." This is what Paul meant by living in the flesh, and why he so forcefully exhorted the Galatians to move **from** living that way **to** living in the Spirit.

❧❧

We have taken some space in this chapter to explore the problem Paul addressed in Galatia, and to see what he understood the solution to be. Now, however, we must take what we have learned from the Galatians' from/to movement and apply it to our movement today. One insightful way to do this is to consider Thomas Merton's perspective, which essentially describes the flesh/Spirit reality of Galatians and applies it to living today. Merton described living in the flesh as living as a false self; he described living in the Spirit as living as a true self. He wrote: "A man cannot enter into the deepest center of himself and pass through that center into God, unless he is able to pass entirely out of himself and empty himself and give himself to other people in the purity of a selfless love."[6]

The crucial thing to note in Merton's statement (as was true for Paul's writing as well) is that we do not jettison the self. Rather, we "pass entirely out of" the self, which means that we do not allow the self to define, control, or direct us. As E. Stanley Jones put it, we experience a "deliverance from self-centered preoccupation."[7] Theologically, this means moving the ego from the center to the circumference, not cancelling the ego but rather consecrating the ego to God alone. Such deliverance is moving from living a self-oriented life to a Spirit-oriented life, moving from selfishness to surrender. Living in the Spirit (i.e., living in our true self) is freedom (Gal 5:1). It is freedom from believing (to use the poet's

6. Thomas Merton, *New Seeds of Contemplation* (New Directions, 1961), 64.

7. Jones, *Growing Spirituality*, 19 (Week 3, Thursday). Three writers provide especially important insights that expand Merton's false self/true self concept: (1) James Finley, *Merton's Palace of Nowhere: A Search for God through Awareness of the True Self* (Ave Maria Press, 1978); (2) M. Robert Mulholland Jr., *The Deeper Journey: The Spirituality of Discovering Your True Self* (InterVarsity Press, 2006); and (3) Richard Rohr, *Falling Upward: A Spirituality for the Two Halves of Life* (Jossey-Bass, 2011).

words) that we are the masters of our fates and the captains of our souls, to believing that we live, move, and have our being in God (Acts 17:28). Living in the Spirit is freedom from the deadly deceptions of legalism and moving into the divine deliverances made possible by grace.

With the flesh/Spirit, false self/true self idea in place, we are now ready to look at the metaphor of the journey and describe how the spiritual life unfolds. When we understand the spiritual life as a journey, then we respond to grace in ever-expanding, never-ending ways. We activate the from/to movement, which is essential if we are to live abundantly. Such a movement moves us into increasing Christian maturity. The earliest Christians understood this, referring to themselves as "followers of the way" before they were called Christians. They were followers of Jesus, who said, "I am the Way"—the incarnation of ancient wisdom and the means to live authentically and abundantly in that wisdom.[8]

We step onto the path through *metanoia*, through repentance. Sadly, repentance has been so linked to sin that we miss the word's broader meaning. Repentance means having a larger perspective about life—the very thing we describe as living beyond the flesh and into the Spirit. When Jesus called people to repent, he was asking them, "Are you willing to look at life in a new way?" And when he invited them to follow him, he was asking them, "If so, do you believe I can show you that new way?" In Matthew's Gospel, Jesus took people who said "Yes" to both questions to a mountain outside Capernaum and taught them about this new life, in what we today call the Sermon on the Mount, specifically

---

8. Cynthia Bourgeault's book, *The Wisdom Jesus* (Shambala Publications, 2008), has helped shape my understanding of Christ and Christianity. Prior to that, E. Stanley Jones's *The Way* (Abingdon Press, 1946) opened me to the idea, giving substantial and ongoing shape to it.

the Beatitudes with which Jesus began his sermon. In the style of a wisdom teacher, Jesus used the Beatitudes to describe the from/to journey—the movement from egotism to imago, from living in the flesh to living in the Spirit, from living by the dictates of the false self to living by the design of the true self.

Woven into the journey/pathway metaphor is the idea of a descent/ascent movement.[9] Every major religion understands the path of life to include descent and ascent. That is, if we are to live as God intends, we must move downward from one mountain and then upward to another—what David Brooks has recently described as moving from the first mountain to a second one.[10] The idea that descent is the initial movement is because using the word *descent* is a way of saying that we must come "down" from the pinnacle of pride created by the false self and by self-righteousness. E. Stanley Jones wrote about the idea of decent as, "We have to reverse our values before we can get new ones."[11]

The first three Beatitudes illustrate the path of descent, the movement away from egotism.[12] They lead us down from the mountain of pride through renunciation ("poor in spirit"), through lament for having lived selfishly ("mourn"), and into a humility disposed toward obedience ("meek"). The first three

9. Other pairings in scripture communicate the same idea: dying/rising (Rom 6:5), putting off/putting on (Col 3:5-17), retreating/advancing (Mark 6:31), and pruning/increasing (John 15:2).

10. David Brooks, *The Second Mountain* (Random House, 2019).

11. Jones, *Growing Spirituality*, 14 (Week 2, Saturday).

12. There are many good books about the Beatitudes. I particularly recommend these: (1) Susan Muto, *Blessings That Make Us Be* (Crossroad Publishing, 1982); (2) John Dear, *The Beatitudes of Peace* (Twenty-Third Publications, 2016); and (3) Richard Rohr, *Jesus's Plan for a New World* (St. Anthony Messenger Press, 2011). These provide a panoramic view of the Beatitudes, showing how they are life-giving in many ways. Eugene Peterson applies the Beatitudes to the life and work of clergy in *The Contemplative Pastor* (Word Publishing, 1989).

Beatitudes incline our hearts toward surrender, sorrow, and self-consecration. They empty us of the self so that we can be filled with the Spirit.[13] Barbara Brown Taylor described descent in a powerful way: "You only need to lose track of who you are, or who you thought you were supposed to be, so that you end up lying flat on the dirt floor basement of your heart. Do this, Jesus says, and you will live."[14]

The fourth Beatitude is the pivot point, simultaneously ending the descent motif and initiating the ascent into abundant life: hungering and thirsting for righteousness (Matt 5:6). In our hungering and thirsting we recognize both our problem and our need. Our problem is that we have fed too long (to use Paul's words) on the flesh; our need is to be fed by the Spirit. The word that describes the end of the old way of life and the beginning of the new way is *longing*, which takes us right back to Nicodemus and why he came to Jesus. Nicodemus had come to the pivot point—to the place of hungering and thirsting for righteousness, and he believed it meant feeding on God in new ways, in ways his previous religious experience had not provided.

The final four Beatitudes illustrate the ascent: the way of showing compassion ("merciful"), having a singular motive ("pure in heart"), working for the establishment of *shalom* ("peace-making"), and finding the strength necessary to endure harassment ("persecution for righteousness sake"). With these qualities operating within us, the rest of the Sermon on the Mount shows what the inward and outward expressions of true spirituality are. They are

13. E. Stanley Jones's book, *Victory Through Surrender* (Abingdon Press, 1966) is one of the best books for understanding and experiencing the movement away from self-centeredness.

14. Barbara Brown Taylor, *Leaving Church: A Memoir of Faith* (HarperOne, 2006), xiii.

nothing other, Jesus said, than transformation—moving from the old creation (of the self) to the new creation (of the Spirit) by living "in Christ" (2 Cor 5:17). The old passes away, and the new creation comes.

Richard Rohr summarized everything we have been looking at as "The Pattern of Spiritual Transformation": order, disorder, reorder.[15] By **order**, Rohr meant the status-quo realities by which the ego has shaped us. As I have written above, not all of the realities are bad. They are just insufficient. They will not take us where we once thought they would. They cannot give us the life we once believed they could. To return to Paul's metaphor, living by this egoic order is living in the flesh. **Disorder** ensues. We become dissatisfied, perhaps even disillusioned because we have spent a lot of time, energy, and even money creating the first order. But now, we know we must change if we are ever to experience the life we long for. The ego resists this, trying to convince us to continue to stay in the first order and just "work harder" (performance oriented) to make it work. Now, however, there is another voice telling us that doing this will only take us farther away from the goal and bring us into greater exhaustion and discouragement. This new voice says, "There is another way to look at life." If we pay attention to that new voice, we enter into **reorder**. Rohr called this "the life on the other side of death, the victory on the other side of failure, the joy on the other side of the pains of childbirth."[16] The biblical word for it is *salvation*—not just going to heaven when we die, but living abundantly while we're here on earth.

---

15. Richard Rohr, *The Universal Christ* (Convergent Books, 2019), 243–48.
16. Rohr, *The Universal Christ*, 245.

In the Beatitudes, Jesus described a reordered life as one of blessedness, and the Greek word Jesus uses is *makarios*.[17] *Makarios* is a description of highest joy, greatest fulfillment, and ultimate meaning—a word that is unaltered by the winds of circumstance, a quality of life that is constant. *Makarios* connotes a dimension of life about which we could say, "Look no further; this is the life you have always wanted, the life you are made for." This word certainly has heavenly dimensions, but it is also about the life lived here and now. *Makarios* is what Nicodemus was longing for when he came to Jesus by night, and it's what the Galatians missed by trying to live by the law instead of by grace. It's what Merton meant by living in congruence with our true self; it is living a blessed life.

Paul's letter to the Galatians fits fully into the picture we have described. The flesh/Spirit movement has a clear "before-and-after" quality. Paul describes the movement in Galatians 5:16-26, beginning with characteristics of living by selfish desires (v. 19-21) and moving into the qualities of life produced in us by the Holy Spirit (v. 22-24). These two ways of living "are opposed to each other," Paul writes (v. 17), and it is impossible to blend them into a have-your-cake-and-eat-it-too lifestyle. Nothing other than a radical departure **from** living in the flesh to a foundational formation **to** living in the Spirit will suffice. Living in the Spirit is nothing other than movement from death to life.

We have spent a fair amount of space describing the life God intends for us and the movement we make in response to grace in order to live that life. This is a foundational chapter for this book, but it is also the port of entry into abundant living. Using Paul's

---

17. Mounce, *Complete Expository Dictionary of Old and New Testament Words*, 69.

words in Galatians, the movement from the flesh to the Spirit is necessary if we are to experience the life God has in mind for us. That reality, however, requires knowing if we are moving in the right direction. It is possible to be moving, but not moving in a formative way. No matter how much we study scripture and theology, the movement becomes intensely personal and practical. The question, then, is: How can I know if I am on the way? There is no one-size-fits-all answer to this question. It is important to remember that each of us is unique, but we also share in a universal *imago dei*. It is possible to explore the question along common lines, and when we do so, some important things emerge.

First, we discern the validity of our movement by walking in a relaxed manner.[18] Thomas Keating rightly noted that the two great temptations in finding and following our spiritual path are overworking and overthinking.[19] Overworking turns spiritual formation in to a never-ending quest for some practice that will "bring it all together" and "make it happen." Overworking can drive us from book to book (even this one) and workshop to workshop, searching for something additional to try. The essence of the spiritual life, however, is not trying; it is trusting. Simply put, we do not create the life we long for; that life already exists. We enter it. Thomas Merton rightly observed that there is a deformative activism in some versions of spirituality, an activism he referred to as "violence," which we do to ourselves and, in turn, inflict upon others.[20]

---

18. The idea of walking "in a relaxed manner" became a formative metaphor for me after reading Joyce Rupp's book, *Walk in a Relaxed Manner* (Orbis Books, 2005), which recounts her walk along the Camino de Santiago (Spain) with a friend.

19. Thomas Keating, "A Great Presence Arises," *Contemplative Outreach News*, vol. 36, no. 2 (June 2019): 1.

20. Thomas Merton, *Conjectures of a Guilty Bystander* (Image Books, 1968), 86.

Legalism is fertile ground for growing this kind of thing. That's why Paul was so concerned when legalism raised its ugly head again in Galatia. There is no end to the making of rules, or to the creation of communities of judges who use regulations to validate their own righteousness (actually, their self-righteousness) and to question others' righteousness through a never-ending list of commandments. The more rules there are, the harder people must work to know the rules and to keep them. The more regulations there are, the more we become strangers to grace.[21] Paul said that a spirituality that overworks things is futile; no one will be made righteous that way (Gal 2:16).

Along with overworking things, we also face the temptation to overthink things. Even this chapter has gone into some detail about the movement from flesh to Spirit, and it would be easy to go even farther. I spent my years of professional ministry in theological education, where almost every day we explored things in great detail. There is nothing intrinsically evil in this; the problem comes when we move into complexification—that is, the never-ending addition of specifics to the point of creating unnecessary detail. In some ways, this is exactly what happened when the original version of the law expanded into over six hundred applications. Jesus cut through religious complexification and said that the entire law and all the prophets hung on two commands: love God and love others as yourself. Complexification undermines simplicity with a "more is better" (quantified) view of the spiritual life.

There is another problem, however, with complexification in that it reaches a point where only "the experts" can make sense of

---

21. Philip Yancey, *Vanishing Grace* (Zondervan, 2018). After surveying the contemporary Christian landscape, Yancey concluded that the absence of grace was deforming Christians. Like Paul, Yancey wrote about that peril and the means for restoring grace to the center of faith.

things and tell the rest of us what's true. Complexification creates a guild of religious leaders who are active and a mass of ordinary folks who become passive regarding their own formation. Complexification is what the Judaisers in Galatia thrived on: "We alone know the truth. We alone have the light. We alone can tell you what the ways of God are and how you must live them in order for God to love you." Paul looked at this situation and exclaimed to the Galatian Christians, "You irrational Galatians! Who put a spell on you?" (Gal 3:1). The answer was those who persuaded them to abandon grace and return to their own human efforts.

So, we must reject overworking and overthinking our spirituality. The movement we are describing in this chapter is one from trying to trusting, one of moving into a reliance on God rather than on ourselves and our systems. This movement renounces human effort and is increasingly receptive to the Spirit. Again, however, we must understand what this means. As I have grown older in age and in faith, I have come to believe such a movement is what Frederick Buechner meant when he wrote, "Listen to your life" and what Parker Palmer meant when he wrote, "Let your life speak."[22] The movement into spiritual life is believing we are already in it, and our advancement in it is essentially taking our lives as seriously as God takes them—that is, believing God is more interested in our living abundantly than we are. It is what Jesus and others since him have called living from the heart.[23]

---

22. Frederick Buechner, *Now and Then* (Harper & Row, 1983), 92. Parker Palmer, *Let Your Life Speak* (Jossey-Bass, 2000).

23. I wrote about this idea in relation to the Wesleyan tradition in, *Prayer and Devotional Life of United Methodists* (Abingdon Press, 1999). Although the book was part of a United Methodist series, you do not have to be a United Methodist in order to glean insights from it.

Parker Palmer invites us into this reality by writing, "Before you tell your life what you intend to do with it, listen for what it intends to do with you."[24] There is no such thing as an insignificant life. There is no such thing as a silent life. Saint Francis said that God does cartwheels in creation, and you and I are parts of that creation. God delights in us and dances in us. Our call (and yes, it is a calling, a vocation) is to hear the music and dance with it. Because we are living souls we are able to do both things (Gen 2:7).

I have come to believe this is precisely what Jesus invited people to do when he beckoned them to ask, seek, and knock. Each word is a means for listening to our lives, a means for paying attention to the Message and living a response to it. All three words define us as explorers in a world that already exists, learners (a key meaning of the world *disciple*) in God's school, which is already in session. Each word enhances exploration in a particular way.

By asking, we are looking at our lives and saying: "What is there about me that is worth paying attention to?" Sadly, some mistakenly denigrate their humanity, going so far as to ascribe their sinfulness to it—"Don't blame me. I am only human." When we look at ourselves in this way and use it to scapegoat our faults and failures, then we cut ourselves off from a primary pathway for moving from the flesh into the Spirit. Our first need is not to deny our humanity, but rather to develop it. Our fundamental problem is not that we are human, it is that we are not human enough![25]

---

24. Palmer, *Let Your Life Speak*, 3.

25. Jean Vanier helped me see the necessity of claiming our humanity as a kind of "first conversion" in *Becoming Human* (Paulist Press, 1998). I have come to believe that if we embrace what Vanier says in this book, then we would be well on our way to living abundantly. Our world would be a different place if we lived in the ways he describes.

When we ask, we raise the essential question about what being human means to us.

Being human means paying attention to our gender, identity, orientation, race, ethnicity, cultural context, location, community, network of relationships, job, and so on. Every facet of life has something to offer us. Everything belongs.[26] There is a psychology of spiritual growth that explores the stages of human development to glean insights about maturing the spiritual life.[27] In doing so, people sometimes ask about the place and value of surveys, instruments, and inventories.[28] My answer is: "They are helpful if they help you think more about your life; they are unhelpful if you think they tell you who you are." Each one of us is more than how each is assessed, but assessments can be a form of exploration, a means for thinking about things we might not otherwise have considered. In the process of asking and assessing we discover our gifts of creation and re-creation.[29]

In historic Christian spirituality, asking is often referred to as the practice of self-examination. Asking uses questions to open doors into discernment and to shed brighter light on our pathways. John Wesley and the early Methodists, for example, had general questions that they asked every morning and evening (as well as specific questions for each day of the week). These

26. Richard Rohr's book, *Everything Belongs* (Crossroad, 1999), opens the way for seeing this.

27. Benedict Groeschel's *Spiritual Passages: The Psychology of Spiritual Development* (Crossroad, 1986) provides significant connections between our humanity and our spirituality.

28. Examples of these instruments are the Myers-Briggs Personality Type Inventory, the Enneagram, and various spiritual-gifts inventories.

29. M. Robert Mulholland's *Invitation to a Journey: A Road Map for Spiritual Formation* (InterVarsity Press, 1993) has several helpful chapters about the place of our humanity in our spirituality (45–73).

questions heightened their attentiveness; here are some examples of the general questions:

- Am I consciously or unconsciously creating the impression that I am better than I really am? In other words, am I a hypocrite?

- Am I honest in all my acts and words, or do I exaggerate?

- Can I be trusted?

- Do I pray about the money I spend?

- Do I insist upon something about which my conscience is uneasy?

- Am I defeated in any part of my life?

- Am I jealous, impure, critical, irritable, touchy, or distrustful?

- Am I proud?

- Do I thank God that I am not as other people, especially as the Pharisees did who despised the publican?[30]

The point of self-examination is that it is an expression of asking that yields insights by which we can grow, both by continuing to cultivate what bears fruit and by "weeding out" what is not. This is one way in which we listen to our lives, but as we listen, we must be careful not to fall prey to scrupulosity—that is, to a manifestation of complexification that not only goes beyond what is reasonable but also generates false guilt. Some people are prone to this, and using questions in such a way that leads to these

---

30. A complete list of questions is found in Wesley's treatise, *A Collection of Forms of Prayer for Every Day in the Week* (1733). Frederick Gill republished them in, *John Wesley's Prayers* (Abingdon Press, 1951). David deSilva revised and updated the collection in *Praying with John Wesley* (Discipleship Resources, 2001).

things is deformative. Asking is about insight, and we must always ask in the atmosphere of grace, where even things that make us uncomfortable can be bridges to a better way of living.

Asking moves into seeking. The simple fact is that when we sincerely inquire about our spiritual life, a plethora of things comes to mind—too many things for us to deal with in a formative way. Asking is helpful when it enables us to think widely and deeply about our lives, but it is unhelpful when it moves us to feeling overwhelmed. When you find yourself thinking, "There's too much here. I can never deal with this," then you know you have asked too much. You know it is time to move beyond asking and into seeking.

Seeking is trusting the Spirit to move us toward the things that matter most for the growth of our spiritual life in the present moment. Good spiritual directors tell us that, while we may have a long list of "good things to do" to grow in our spiritual life, we can only manage a few at a time. Seeking is the stage of movement in which we pray, "God, what would you have me do at this time in my life to grow in your grace?" Almost always, the longer list of options is reduced to a smaller number (i.e., two or three) of things to pay particular attention to at the moment. One of the facts of spiritual formation is that we grow little-by-little and step-by-step, not in leaps and bounds. We grow in bits, not in bulk. We grow by tending to the things that call for our attention here and now.

A simple question I have asked others over the years is: "So, what's on your mind?" Almost always, they can tell me. There is something that has surfaced, something that stands out among the laundry list of possibilities, something that invites them to take action. E. Stanley Jones called it receiving our marching orders. To move from asking to seeking is to move from the many to the few. It is deciding to set up shop in a particular area of life. Seeking does not second guess; that is, seeking wastes no time speculating why something has popped up and something else has not. Seeking accepts "what is" and uses it as a specific agenda to explore growing in the grace and knowledge of Jesus Christ. We move in relation to what moves us.

Furthermore, our seeking turns into knocking. We locate ourselves before a particular thing and we knock on its door, realizing that we have much to discover. Knocking allows the door to open so that we can enter the house of a particular inclination and dwell there. Knocking is a combination of confidence and patience—confidence that we have indeed landed on something important, and patience that we need not rush the process in order to harvest the fruit of our exploration. Jesus said, "Knock and the door will be opened" (Matt 7:7). God is not a reluctant host, but rather is one who says, "Come in and sit a spell." This is what I meant earlier when I described the journey as walking in a relaxed manner. Cultivating the spiritual life is never frenetic; it is never aimed at producing a quick fix.

The ask, seek, and knock movement is almost always in relation to our current circumstance and present spiritual season. With respect to our current circumstances, the movement means owning the reality of whether we are currently in order, disorder, or reorder. If we are in a time of order, then what is stirring in us that seems to beckon us to move into something new? If we are in a time of disorder, then are we willing to view the turmoil as a "sifting and sorting" so that the chaff can be separated from the wheat? If we are in a time of reorder, are we willing to let the new fruit grow agriculturally (i.e., first the blade, then the ear, then

the full corn) rather than artificially? In each condition we usually find that we are invited to concentrate on something specific
(not hypothetical), and something routine (not spectacular). This
is what the saints have often called "ordinary holiness." Eugene
Peterson captured this in his translation of Romans 12:1 in *The
Message*:

> So, here's what I want you to do, God helping you: Take your ev-
> eryday, ordinary life—your sleeping, eating, going-to-work, and
> walking-around life—and place it before God as an offering.

In the domain of the simple, the treasures of the spiritual life are
found. Anyone can be knocked off his or her feet by a blinding
light or a mountain-top experience—and those do happen on the
journey. Where we grow most, however, is in being attentive to
the "still, small voice," to the whispers of grace that say, "This is
the way, walk in it" (Isa 30:21).

Our current realities, our here-and-now moments, are always
in relation to the particular season of life in which we live. We
grow in our spiritual life within the context of our age and stage of
life. Parker Palmer wrote about this in a very helpful way, pointing
out that the spiritual journey is never-ending and that we "live the
questions" throughout our lives.[31] The kinds of questions noted
above sound different at different stages. The current realities of
today are not identical to those of the past. The writer of Ecclesi-
astes had this in mind when he wrote, "There's a season for everything, and a time for every matter under the heavens" (Eccl 3:1).

I find it very beneficial to look at the spiritual life as "sea-
sonal" growth. Springtime is a time in our souls when new life

---

31. Palmer, *Let Your Life Speak*, 95. Palmer provides an excellent introduction
to the seasons of the spiritual life and how we can live well in each of them.

is emerging; it is a season to pay attention to buds of intuition and sprouts of possibility. Summertime then brings them into a crescendo of life. In the summer we experience a spirituality of abundance. In the fall things begin to slow down and some things fall by the wayside. Autumn, however, is one of the most beautiful seasons because of its colors and quietude. Then comes winter, which, far from being a "dead time" in the spiritual life, is the season when life goes underground—when the most important thing about spirituality is not having or doing, but *being*. Winter enables us to see what things matter most and find joy tending to them.

These seasons are part of the human lifecycle. I am in the late stages of fall and perhaps the early stages of winter, what the Bible calls becoming an elder. It is indeed a time of beauty and simplification, a quieter and slower time, but is also one that teaches me that abundant life is not a quality only for one or two seasons of life, but for every season. Abundant living has no expiration date!

Moving into wider and deeper dimensions of the spiritual life is, in the end, moving into the love. We will explore this further through Paul's reference to the fruit of the Spirit. For this chapter, however, moving into love is our way of saying what Paul said elsewhere, "the greatest of these is love" (1 Cor 13:13). We are made by love, for love. Every detail of the movement from flesh to Spirit is about moving increasingly into love. The rest of this book is an invitation to do just this. Thomas Merton wrote eloquently about this: "Love is the reason for my existence, for God is love. Love is my true identity. Selflessness is my true self. Love is my true character. Love is my name."[32] This is the movement—the journey into love. There is no other.

---

32.   Merton, *New Seeds of Contemplation*, 60.

Chapter Three

The Atmosphere

Things grow best when the atmosphere is good, when the season is right and the temperature, soil, nutrients, water, and all the rest enhance natural growth. Things thrive when the atmosphere is at its best, and the spiritual life is the same. We are made for growth, but we grow best in a formative atmosphere. Paul described this idea in three words: "My little children" (Gal 4:19). The movement we looked at in the last chapter, from living in the flesh to living in the Spirit, occurs in a relational atmosphere. By examining the phrase "my little children," we learn important truths about Paul and about the Galatians. We can then transfer what we learn to the formative relationship that enhances our life in Christ today.

Beginning with Paul himself, we immediately see endearment. Paul's tone was both parental and pastoral. This tone was based on the fact that he had spent time in Galatia (Acts 13–14), coming to know and love the people there. Those days together provided the necessary basis for him to re-enter their lives through his letter and to exhort them not to abandon the Christian journey, which they had only recently begun. Similarly, today, spiritual formation occurs best in a relational atmosphere, not a transactional one. As Parker Palmer has noted, the best teachers do not teach subjects as much as they teach themselves. He writes: "We teach who we are."[1] Paul clearly did this in his letter to the Galatians. The autobiographical nature of his letter tells us some very important aspects about Paul, and about any good spiritual guide.

First, Paul was transparent. He most likely did not write anything in the letter that the Galatians did not already know, but by repeating certain truths, Paul was demonstrating that his life was an open book. He was not writing abstract theology; he was sharing personal experience—experience that had enlivened him in ways that nothing else had. He was not sharing a topic; he was sharing himself.

I taught for over thirty years, but it soon became clear that I was not so much teaching a course as I was communicating an experience. I quickly discovered that formative teaching is sharing content that had first entered me before I passed it on to students. Formative teachers stand inside the circle of their content. Parker Palmer calls this courageous teaching because it "joins self and subject and students in the fabric of life."[2] This is exactly the kind of teaching Paul engaged in with the Galatians. It took courage for him to be as honest as he needed to be in what he wrote. This courage was possible because of the relationship that existed between Paul and the Galatians. He had already made many deposits into their lives; now, he could make some withdrawals without fear of destroying the relationship.

Our spiritual life thrives in an atmosphere where heart-to-heart openness is present, but is diminished when we believe we

---

1. Parker Palmer, *The Courage to Teach* (Jossey-Bass, 1998), 1.
2. Palmer, *The Courage to Teach*, 11.

are permitted only to affirm the status quo, not to question it. The spiritual life thrives in an atmosphere where questions are welcomed, not as occasions for "experts" to give answers, but as moments for fellow pilgrims to go beneath the surface of their experiences. Deep teaching does not mean making things more complex, but rather making them more real (authentic and desirable) through sharing lived experience. Paul surely did this in his letter to the Galatians, and transparency remains part of the formative atmosphere in which our spiritual life grows.

Second, Paul declared his integrity. Good teachers must exemplify integrity in general, but in Paul's case the need to declare his integrity was especially important because it was his character that the Judaisers were undermining. Their attempt could be summarized like this: "Paul's message lacks credibility because his life lacks character." That is always a damning charge whenever it is made. In Paul's case, it was an allegation that threatened to undermine and undo everything he had accomplished with the Galatians. He spent quite a bit of time in the letter disputing the false claim made against him by proving the genuineness of his character.

The link between leadership and character cannot be severed without deformative consequences. Spiritual guides must be on the path themselves if they are to counsel others about being on it. In fact, the word *integrity* emerges from the ideas of integration and wholeness. Paul understood this, and so must we. In various ways, Paul used his letter to the Galatians to say, "You cannot separate me from the message I have shared with you." He was a living manifestation of the letter. Thomas Aquinas called this *tradere contemplativa*, which means to share the fruits of one's own contemplation.[3] Contemplation opens us to realities beneath the surface level, and from that place of intuitive insight, a door opens for sharing our experiences. In this sense, Paul was truly an apostle, someone sent to tell others what he had seen and heard (Acts 4:20).

At this point it is essential to clarify that integrity does not mean total flawlessness, which is a psychological malady, not a spiritual virtue. Paul was able to differentiate between his foundational character and his ongoing maturation in faith. He never lived beyond humility, always remembering the extent to which he had sinned against the very gospel he had been called to declare (1 Tim 1:15). Nor did he minister personally to others or write letters as one who had arrived, but only as one who, like them, was on the way toward greater healing and wholeness (Phil 3:14). This tone saturated his letter to the Galatians, binding Paul to his siblings in Christ in an empathetic way.

Third, Paul was a participant in the message he was asking the Galatians to embrace. This has already been seen in the previous points about transparency and integrity. It bears emphasizing, however, both in what we see in Paul and also in what must be present in formative spiritual guidance today. The parental and pastoral tone of the letter to the Galatians shows that Paul was on the journey with them. The best teaching and spiritual guidance come from those who are learning and being guided. Spiritual formation is advanced by people who are themselves being formed.

In my early years as a Christian, I participated in a variety of small-group experiences. The quality of those experiences largely revolved around the disposition of the group leader. Also, they tended to fall into two categories. The first kind of leader was the

3. Maria Lichtmann, *The Teacher's Way* (Paulist Press, 2005), 7.

one whose content and tone communicated this message to the rest of the group members: "My aim is to disciple you in ways that will eventually make you as spiritual as I am." From that pedestal, these group leaders taught as if they were a "graduate" in the school of spiritual maturity, commending resources and practices they were already doing. Without ever actually saying it out loud, the unspoken lesson was to commit ourselves to becoming the leader's clones. We would know we had arrived when we were like our leader. I must say that I learned a lot in these kinds of groups because I had a lot to learn, but I missed the *telos*—the ultimate purpose—of group formation: to be like Christ.

The true purpose came through the second kinds of leaders, those who were on the journey with us, not at the end waiting for the rest of us to catch up. To be sure, these leaders were "ahead" of us (and there's nothing wrong with receiving guidance from people who are farther along on the path than you are), but their spirit was participatory, not declaratory. Rather than developing a discipling style that said, "become like me," they were engaged with us in a process that said, "become like Christ." Looking back, I can see a world of difference between the self-referent leader and the Christ-referent one.

Paul fell into the second category because his desire was for Christ to be formed in the Galatians (4:19). Later in *Life in Christ* we will further explore the riches of this verse but, for now, this verse shines light on the kind of spiritual leader and guide Paul was trying to be and the way we must seek to be as we lead and guide others. Parker Palmer describes the same idea this way: "Education is to guide students on an inner journey toward more truthful ways of seeing and being in the world."[4] This is the kind

---

4. Palmer, *The Courage to Teach*, 6.

of spiritual formation happening in Paul's letter to the Galatians, precisely because it was the spirit with which he taught them and wrote to them, and because their challenge was to discern how best to see and be in the world where they lived. As we have seen, for Paul, the best way was to live is in the Spirit, not in the flesh. He was participating with them in that aim, working out his own salvation just as he was encouraging them to do (Phil 2:12).

Fourth, we detect the tone of hope in Paul's writing. Paul truly believed that if the Galatians lived God's way, then they would live with God's blessing. He believed they had been created for that very purpose. Paul would have agreed with E. Stanley Jones that the Christian way is built into our very existence. We cannot escape this reality; we can only abandon it.[5]

Hope is the atmosphere that says that our current reality is not the final word. By expressing his concern to the Galatians, Paul envisioned a way for them to return to life in the Spirit as they had come to know it when he was with them. His hope was not naïve. There were formidable obstacles, and he mentions them all the way to the end of the letter. However, Paul's conviction was that it is always possible to overcome internal and external resistance and return to our life in Christ. As he wrote the letter, he held on to the hope that the Galatians would be restored to life in the Spirit and renewed in their life in Christ.

It is difficult to underestimate the importance of hope for those who serve as spiritual guides for others. When we lose hope that those for whom we care will ever be different, we withdraw from the relationship, whether others see it or not. We become absent even in our presence. Our investment is reduced, our

---

5. E. Stanley Jones, *The Way* (Abingdon Press, 1946), 6 (Week One, Friday).

devotion is diminished. Hope is necessary if we are to continue to speak and act in Jesus's name.

When I write like this, I think of Dorothy Day. She accepted God's call to be deeply involved in the lives of people who were often hopeless, people who had given up on themselves and saw little potential to be different. Sadly, she observed priests in the church who "underestimate the capacity of their penitents for the spiritual life and gave minimum instruction."[6] Far from pointing her finger at others, however, she acknowledged that being "involved in too many problems at home, one is apt to lose sight of the hopeful and joyful."[7] She often prayed that she would not lose hope.

The fact that Paul wrote the letter to the Galatians is the sign that he had not lost hope. His disposition toward the Galatians provided them with the basis to receive his letter and take his admonition to heart. His transparency, integrity, participation, and hope sent this message: "I know you can do this. I know it!" In turn, his demeanor produced in them key ingredients they needed in order to return to life in the Spirit.

In his letter, we see a number of formative factors. First, the Galatians were objects of Paul's affection. They knew he loved them, even when he had to speak strong words to them. If they were to return to life in the Spirit, then they would most likely do it knowing they were loved, first of all by God and second of all by Paul. There are times that we change only when the Spirit-human combination of love assures us that we are loved. Without the assurance of God's love, we may mistake the love of others for

---

6. Robert Ellsberg, *The Duty of Delight: The Diaries of Dorothy Day*, abridged ed. (Image Books, 2011), loc 5922.

7. Ellsberg, *The Duty of Delight*, loc 5914.

sentimentality. Without others' love, however, we may perceive God's love as a good theory, but one that never seems to happen in actual practice. When God's love and others' love combine, then we experience the affection within which change can occur.

Second, the Galatians knew they were secure. By reading the words *my little children*, they knew Paul was not going to abandon them. To be sure, he was disappointed, and deeply so (see Gal 1:6), but the fact that he was writing to them, rather than writing them off, was enough to let them know their relationship was not in jeopardy. Through Paul's parental and pastoral care, they experienced God's love, which would not let them go. Paul's letter was not a threat (i.e., "do this, or else"); rather, it was a promise that he would remain with them until they came to their senses and laid new hold on life in the Spirit. They were secure and, in such security, change is always possible.

Third, they were invited to change within the context of reality. That is, returning to life in the Spirit would not be easy. We will look at this in more detail in the next chapter; for now, it is important to remember that spiritualty is reality. It is not complex, but neither is it easy. There is nothing to be gained, and there is much to be lost, if we profess to be someone we are not—if we allege to be at a stage in the spiritual life in which we do not inhabit. Reality will not always comfort us, but it will always awaken us. Unreality keeps us asleep in a spiritual la-la land.

Fourth, the Galatians were challenged to change within the atmosphere of encouragement. Here, I use the word *encouragement* in its literal meaning, which is to live with the heightened resolve that change is possible. Encouragement is courage blended with confidence. When we seek to grow in the spiritual life, it is important that we feel encouraged to do so. On the surface, we often find ourselves thinking, "It's not worth it." Encouragement is what takes us beyond our first impressions into a deeper conviction that who we desire to be through life in Christ is worth desiring. We have turned it into a little song, "I have decided to follow Jesus. No turning back."

Finally, Paul encouraged the Galatians to grow little-by-little. We will see this in greater detail when we explore the word *formed* in chapter six. This is how Paul described the Galatians' recovery of life in the Spirit. For now, it is enough to think of it the way I did when my dad measured my growth. Jesus used a similar metaphor from agriculture, where the wheat grows little-by-little until it is ready to be harvested. We grow like this in the spiritual life as well. This is why it is important not to confuse one stage of our formation with the totality of it, why it is important to keep growing. We are always becoming, and Thomas Merton captured this idea in *Contemplative Prayer*: "We do not want to be beginners. But let us be convinced of the fact that we will never be anything else but beginners all our days."[8]

Throughout the years of my seminary teaching, I tried to say the same thing to my students. If any are reading this book, they will recall me saying on more than one occasion, "If I could, I would change the name of the degree many of you will receive: Master of Divinity. That is a terrible name for a theological degree. We never 'master' divinity. We are supposed to be mastered by divinity." There is nothing more that I believe more strongly than this, and I see this sentiment coming through in how Paul described life in the Spirit. In our life in Christ, we move from on

8. Thomas Merton, *Contemplative Prayer* (Image Books, 1971), 37. This is the final book he wrote before he died in 1968; it was published posthumously in 1969.

degree of glory to another (2 Cor 3:18). We never graduate; we never arrive.

Putting it all together, both from Paul's perspective as a good spiritual guide and from the Galatians' side as those being guided, we see the formative atmosphere in which life in Christ grows. It is the atmosphere in which we open ourselves up to the ingredients we have highlighted in this chapter—ingredients that enable us to experience the joy of hearing our heavenly Father say, "My, how you've grown!"

The Struggle

F or many years my ministry included air travel, going here and there to preach revivals, speak at conferences, lead retreats, and so on. It was not unusual to board my flight when weather conditions were less than ideal. Almost always, however, I knew that it would only be a little while before the pilot would point the plane's nose upward, and we would leave the clouds behind. We would break through into bright sunshine. All the bad weather would be left behind.

Unfortunately, we have adopted this "nose up, break through, leave the clouds behind" mentality with respect to the spiritual life. In North America in particular, the prosperity gospel (which is actually no gospel) has misled people into believing that somewhere down the line, they will leave the clouds behind, but this is not true. It is not what the Bible teaches. It is not the testimony of the saints across the centuries. Life in Christ inevitably includes struggle, sometimes intense and prolonged struggle. If we leave the reality of struggle out of the story, then we become spiritual "snake oil" salespersons, not spiritual guides.

Thankfully, Paul did not leave this out of his letter to the Galatians. He included it, speaking first about his own struggle upon learning that the believers had taken a U-turn away from grace (Gal 5:4). Paul re-entered the lives of the Galatians because they were headed in the wrong direction. He did so honestly and realistically, writing that he was "going through labor pains" until they got back on track (Gal 4:19). The Greek text is very strong, as are the labor pains they refer to. Paul wanted the Galatians to know that their detour had saddened him in a painful way, and done so at a deep level. His attempted renewal effort via the letter was no small thing.

Reading Paul's words reminded me of another of Paul's testimonies about the struggle he experienced in his faith. At the beginning of his second letter to the Corinthians, he told them about the troubles he and his companions faced in Asia. He pulled no punches in his description of their experience: "We were weighed down with a load of suffering that was so far beyond our strength that we were afraid we might not survive. It certainly seemed to us as if we had gotten the death penalty" (2 Cor 1:8-9). What? God's "thirteenth apostle" writing like this? The one whose conversion is still touted in some circles for its drama, power, and transformation? Paul...despairing of life in general, not just his Christian life? What? Yes, Paul, and those traveling with him. Truth be told, this is true for every follower of Jesus. This is the Christian story.

Simply put, the spiritual life includes struggle, trouble, labor pains, and travail. Lest we forget, these commenced in Jesus himself. Immediately after his baptism, he experienced temptation from Satan himself. Emerging from that and beginning his ministry in Nazareth, the townspeople tried to throw Jesus over a cliff minutes after he delivered his inaugural sermon. After he hit the road, he was then in hot water with the religious leaders before things had barely begun. In fact, the heat never let up, so that even the night he was betrayed, Jesus told three of his disciples, "I'm very sad. It's as if I'm dying" (Matt 26:38). Struggle is the Christian story, and Jesus experienced the struggle himself! How did we ever come to think it would be different for us?

Every Christian passes through the desert on the way to the promised land. Abundant living is not a vaccination against struggle. In fact, it sets the stage for struggle because (as we have already seen) the ego is dethroned, and the way of life we often choose is at cross purposes with the world. We experience struggle internally and externally, personally and socially. When considered against a basic philosophy, "people seek pleasure and avoid pain," we wonder why anyone keeps going with Jesus after they figure this out. Henri Nouwen, who experienced a lot of struggle himself, provides the clue: "All brokenness, and all dying, and all suffering is there to allow you to enter into solidarity with the whole human family, and to give yourselves to others so that your life can bear fruit. God asks you not to have a successful life, but to have a fruitful life."[1]

Life in Christ includes struggle because the whole of life contributes to our spiritual formation. Life is a mixture of pleasant and unpleasant experiences, and all of them contain the means by which we grow. Our predecessors in the faith knew this. We are the ones who have changed the story to make it seem as though only "the positive side" is contributive. As we will see, Paul understood this too, and it comes through in his letter to the Galatians. In classic spiritual formation this idea is described as consolation and desolation. In times of consolation we experience a state of lightness,

---

1. Henri Nouwen, *You Are the Beloved* (Convergent, 2017), 8/9/19.

joy, and freedom. In times of desolation we experience heaviness, sadness, and bondage. Consolation places us in the light; desolation takes us into the darkness.[2] Along with many of you who are reading this, I have experienced both, and I continue to do so.

The important thing to see is that both consolation and desolation are formative parts of the spiritual life. Paul labored to help the Galatians understand this. In our day, Richard Rohr has written a lot about this, making it part of what he means when he writes, "everything belongs."[3] It is the phase of formation that he calls "disorder," which we looked at in chapter two. In other places Rohr refers to it as "necessary suffering."[4]

The challenge of our struggle is simply this: "If we do not transform our pain, we will most assuredly transmit it."[5] In Galatia, the Judaisers had transmitted their pain by transferring their legalism onto the new Christians, making them feel they had done something wrong by following Paul, believing the gospel of grace, and embracing life in the Spirit. Paul knew he could not let the Judaisers prevail. He challenged the Galatians to reverse course and return to life in the Spirit, so that they would not become party to transmitting legalism on to others. To do this would be a struggle because it would require them to say "No" to the Judaisers' group-think approach.[6] An inevitable stage in our spiritual formation is when we have to say "No" to something in order to say "Yes" to something better.

2. Keith Beasley-Topliffe, ed., *The Upper Room Dictionary of Christian Spiritual Formation* (Upper Room Books, 2003), 66.

3. Richard Rohr, *Everything Belongs* (Crossroad, 1999, 2003).

4. Richard Rohr, *A Spring Within Us* (CAC Publications, 2016), weeks 15 and 16.

5. Rohr, *A Spring Within Us*, 119.

6. Rohr, *Everything Belongs*, 94. Rohr says *groupism* is one of legalism's strongest traps and one of the most difficult from which to escape.

When we recognize the consolation/desolation pattern, we can see it running from the beginning of the Bible to the end. We see people in both the Old Testament and the New Testament experiencing struggle. Today, people experience struggle in a variety of ways. Now, we will turn to look at some of the main expressions of struggle.

First, there is spiritual dryness. I think of this as the cycle of ups and downs where God sometimes seems near, and sometimes far away. The severity of this experience varies from everyday "blahs" to extended periods of an intense sense of deprivation.[7] The soul is mysterious, and it often mirrors the circumstances of our lives. When we are experiencing new life, the soul flourishes. When we are in distress, the soul reflects the disorientation.[8] Part of the struggle of the spiritual life is being honest about these fluctuations. John Wesley had a system in his diary for measuring his changes in temperament. By noting them, he could engage the best disciplines (sometimes doing more...sometimes doing less) for restoring his life to better balance and vitality. Other saints, ancient and modern, have found ways to stay in touch with their dryness rather than being in denial about it.

A second manifestation of the struggle is described by an ancient word, *acedia*[9] The early Christian monks (ammas and abbas) who lived in the desert, connected the struggle with the psalmist's

---

7. I wrote about spiritual dryness in more detail in, *Talking in the Dark: Praying When Life Doesn't Make Sense* (Upper Room Books, 2007). In the book, I examine some of the common causes of dryness and how we can move beyond them—at least until it happens again.

8. Bruce Demarest wrote a good book about this pattern: *Seasons of the Soul* (InterVarsity Press, 2009).

9. Kathleen Norris's book, *Acedia and Me* (Riverhead Books, 2008), is an excellent exposition of this struggle, including her very honest writing about it in her life and in her marriage.

phrase, "destruction that ravages at noontime" (Ps 91:6). The description is worth pausing over. First, the psalmist says it happens at noontime—when things are at their brightest and best. This means that *acedia* usually comes surprisingly, when we are not expecting it. The early Christians associated *acedia* with being overly zealous and active in one's faith. It comes close to what we call burnout. Second, *acedia* ravages, which is to say it is more than experiencing spiritual dryness. It is, says the psalmist, destructive. *Acedia* is not merely being "down," it is feeling "down and out." In spiritual dryness the emotions are affected, in *acedia* the will is infected. *Acedia* not only brings sadness, it also brings lethargy. Some have used the word *boredom* to describe *acedia*, but it is the kind of boredom that leads us to believe the best thing we can do is "hang it up" and be done with all this "religion crap" (as one person once described it to me). Evagrius Ponticus, an early-church father, described *acedia* as a weariness of soul that "instills in the heart of the monk a hatred for the place, a hatred for his very way of life, a hatred for manual labor"[10] Needless to say, this is serious.

There is more, however, and the writing of St. John of the Cross describes two additional forms of spiritual struggle: the dark night of the senses and the dark night of the soul. Some have blended the two struggles into one, but John kept them separate, at least technically. When we are in the throes of either one, it may be difficult to distinguish one from the other. The dark night of the senses is a kind of deadness that no amount of spiritual activity can overcome, at least not while we're in the midst of it. Notice that in *acedia*, the emotions are in full swing. This is not so in the dark night of the senses; this is more like a numbness of spirit.

10. Norris, *Acedia and Me*, 24–25.

The dark night of the soul is another form of malaise. It usually includes the dark night of the senses, but it is an even deeper struggle. It is the struggle to trust in the goodness, presence, and activity of God when none of our sensory or spiritual apparatus works. Nothing is incoming. We see it in the psalmist's question, "Why are you hiding your face?" (Ps 44:26), and in other places in the Psalms where equally indicting questions are hurled at the almighty (e.g., Ps 77). We see it in Jesus's anguish in the Garden of Gethsemane where his distress came out like drops of blood while crying out, "Take this cup of suffering away from me" (Matt 26:39), but it didn't happen.

I don't know about you, but even writing these words has led me to the place where I have to bob up for air. The depths to which our spiritual struggles can go are beyond where we normally let our minds go, but they are not beyond the ways we feel from time to time. That's why we must not bypass Paul's "travail," the struggles of the Galatians, or ours. If there is anything to be said, it is this: spirituality is reality. No amount of glossing over it will suffice. In fact, artificiality will only further the downward spiral. So, what then shall we do when we come upon our struggles, whether they fall into any of these illustrative categories, or not? How shall we live in relation to our struggles? We have raised diagnostic questions, but leaving it there is not sufficient. We will experience struggles, and when we do, there are some things we can do to bear up under them.

First, face the facts. Spirituality is reality. No amount of saying "I'm fine" can substitute for those times when we are not fine. In the spiritual life, as elsewhere, honesty is the best policy.[11] Life is

---

11. Philip Yancey's books helped me see the formative benefits of honesty in the midst of struggle. His book, *Where is God When it Hurts?* (rev. ed. [Zondervan, 1996]), is one I continue to turn to and recommend.

uneven. Life is unfair. Life is mystery. For example, looking back on my ministry, I see that some of the people for whom I prayed for healing were healed, yet others were not. Bad things happened to good people and good things to bad people. It is pointless to try to make sense of it all.[12] To wish it were otherwise, and to fight against life, is spiritual fantasy.

Job's friends surrounded him with explanations and exhortations, but it was only when Job surrendered to sovereignty that he moved beyond his suffering. This is why it is important to know we are surrendering to the God of love; otherwise, raw sovereignty would bring us more fear than comfort. If "God is with us" no matter what and in everything, then looking at life honestly brings hope. This is what the writer of Hebrews said faith is: "the reality of what we hope for" (Heb 11:1).

Second, we must understand that spiritual struggle is normal. When I realized this, I saw how the lives of some of the saints who have influenced me most included prolonged and intense periods of struggle. Teresa of Avila wrote that she was spiritually dry for twenty-three years! After reading about her struggle, I began to study it in others and found that people like Charles Spurgeon, Oswald Chambers, E. Stanley Jones, J. B. Phillips, and Mother Teresa struggled while walking their spiritual paths in faith. Nor am I exempt; I have experienced struggle in smaller recurring cycles and in a more intense version around 1985.

When I say that spiritual struggle is normal, I do not mean it is enjoyable. Far from it! Nor do I mean that we should passively accept it (of which I will say more in a moment). What I mean is this: spiritual struggle is survivable. It comes and it goes. When I

---

12. I write about this in *Talking in the Dark: Praying When Life Doesn't Make Sense*.

say that spiritual struggle is normal, I mean, "Strap yourself into the seat and hang on!" Struggle is not an indication that your faith is weak; it is a signal that life is strong. One of the things I appreciate about E. Stanley Jones's writing is the pattern he followed in many of them. Jones began with the topic at hand and why it is important. Then he led his readers through as many as a dozen obstacles that inhibit a quick-and-easy embrace of the subject. Only after a time exploring that reality did he then end his books with the blessings and benefits of living in sync with what he was writing about.

Third, we should seek to know the cause of our struggle. This may sound like I am contradicting what I said earlier about life being a mystery. I am thinking of something else, however. Life is a mystery, but we are not expected to become passive in the face of that mystery. When I get sick, I don't know where I picked up the germ or virus; I only know that I must take the medicine. My job is to cooperate with what the doctor prescribed, knowing that if I do, I will get well. Similarly, seeking to know the cause of my struggle does not eliminate the mystery of it, it only offers me a means of cooperating with God to move beyond it.

A primary cause of struggle is sin. Our spiritual formation must not become sin-focused, but neither can we naively assume that sin has nothing to do with it. So, in seeking to know the cause of my struggles, I ask, "God is there a sin in my life that is causing this?" Often, the Spirit does not convict me of anything, and I move on to consider other causes. Now and again, however, the Spirit responds to my question with, "I'm glad you asked. We need to talk." Even when I do not like it, the conversation turns out to be a very good thing. So, even though we must remain grace-focused in our spirituality, this does not mean assuming sin has nothing to do with our struggles. The ego rises up, even after we are Christians, in all sorts of ways. Sometimes, one of those ways is what's causing the struggle.

I've found that another frequent cause of struggle is what I call affective breakdown. That is, our spiritual life cannot be sustained indefinitely on a "high." No other part of my life stays on the mountain top all the time, and I accept that as normal. I have had to learn to accept that the same is true for my spiritual life. It fluctuates. When I enter times when "God seems far away," I no longer try to whip up some solution. I receive the feeling—as a feeling, not a reality—and take it as a sign to rest and trust. Often, the recovery from this kind of struggle comes through a non-religious activity.

Years ago, I was in my office at the seminary. A student in one of my classes appeared in the doorway, and I motioned for him to come in and sit down. When I asked him why he had come, he replied, "I am experiencing the spiritual dryness you talked about in class today." It turned out that he had a pretty intense bout of it. In fact, he felt as if being in seminary was making things worse instead of better. I remember him saying, "I felt closer to God before I came here" (note: seminary feels like this sometimes).

I asked him, "Was there anything you used to do that helped you feel close to God?" Without hesitating he answered, "Yeah, back in college I enjoyed photography, and I was pretty good at it." But then he added, "I doubt that I could even find my camera now. I guess it's in a box somewhere."

I said, "Find your camera. Buy some film, and go out into the country and take photos with this verse from Psalm 19:1 in mind: 'the heavens declare the glory of God and the firmament shows his handiwork.'" Honestly, he looked at me like I had lost my mind. He was my student, though, and it's difficult to disobey a professor! So, with little enthusiasm showing, he said, "Okay," got up, and walked out. I figured that would be the end of it.

It wasn't. About two weeks later, he appeared in the doorway again, and I could tell at first glance something was different. I didn't have to ask him anything. Instead, he blurted out, "It worked! God came back through my camera!" Of course, he and I knew that was not literally true, for God had never left, but it was experientially true. It was true in a lifegiving way. He asked if he could arrange the photos into a presentation to begin a class session. Of course, I said "Yes." He combined pictures and music in a moving way to show how, indeed, the heavens and earth do glorify God and reveal God's handiwork.

I have taken a bit of space to tell you this story because I believe it is one of the best things we can do when we are struggling spiritually. In a sense I am saying, "Stop struggling. Do something different." God often "returns" through unexpected means. Our spiritual struggles do not yield to white-knuckle attempts to make them go away. More often, they fade away while we are enjoying doing something else. Believe it or not, I have told some people to stop praying and reading the Bible because they were living with a quantified notion of spirituality. They were living with a belief that praying longer and more often, and reading the Bible longer and more often, was the solution when, truth be told, the freneticism was causing the problem. Sometimes, it is best to cut back. Your own soul will let you know when you are hungry again, and it is that sense of hunger you're trying to recover in the first place.

Another cause of struggle can be physical. A friend (let's call him Dan) has given me permission to tell you his story. Not long after coming to seminary, Dan began to struggle. He had responded to a call to ministry while working as an accountant (he was one of many second-career seminarians in those days). When the struggle emerged, Dan's first thought was that he had misunderstood God's call, and that the best thing he could do was drop out of seminary and return to his accounting work. Yet there was something inside that would not let him do that. So, he endured the drought, and worsened. After some weeks of traditional counseling, his therapist suggested that he check into the hospital for a thorough exam. Dan was desperate, willing to try anything. He went that very day. Some of us walked with him through the subsequent days of testing and diagnosis. When the results came in, the doctor found that Dan was missing a key chemical in his brain, the lack of which caused him to feel detached and depressed. The doctor kept him in the hospital a few more days, administering the needed medication, and his struggle ended—but not permanently. Dan has had to stay on the medication ever since and will remain on it for the rest of his life, but it is a regimen that keeps him healthy and happy.

Part of being marvelously and mysteriously made (Ps 139:14) is the delicate balance between our body, soul, and spirit. When that balance is affected, we struggle. It is not surprising, however, that the great physician might choose to give us medicine to restore our health. When this is the case, medication is a gift we use as part of our spiritual formation.

Another cause of struggle is trying to be like someone else. We all have people in our lives whose examples and encouragement have influenced us significantly. When we turn their witness into a mold that we think we must fit into, then God breaks the mold. God is a creator, not a cloner. There is only one "you." Our God-given self is unique and unrepeatable. God brings others into our lives to make us better, not to be like them. God never calls us to live someone else's life, and when we try to do so, we will struggle spiritually.

I'll consider one more cause before concluding. We will struggle spiritually when we do not keep the intake/outflow pattern moving. I mention this because we have become more spiritually consumeristic than is good for us. The "churchianity industry" feeds the temptation to take in without giving out by offering us a never-ending round of resources and events. Even this book runs the risk of being nothing other than "something else to read" in the unceasing attempt to be more spiritual. Hopefully, I have written enough to counteract that challenge, but it is real, nevertheless. The point I make here is that what goes into us is meant to flow out of us. We are blessed to be a blessing. This can be a cliché or it can be the truth—depending on what we do with what we receive. It does us little good to have a wonderful morning devotional about patience, and then go out and yell at the kids and kick the dog. God will not let us get by with a disconnection between what we are receiving and what we are giving. This is another time when cutting back on the "blessing side" may actually make things better. There are times when being nice is better than being spiritual!

There are other causes of spiritual struggle, but these are enough to illustrate the point. Seeking to know the cause of our struggles can help us become co-creators with God in dealing with them. This is part of what Paul meant when he wrote, "carry out your own salvation" (Phil 2:12). This does not mean adopting a self-help spirituality; it means working in concert with the Spirit to move your life in the direction your life must go. Often, we will not know the cause of our struggle and, again, that is because life is mystery. Sometimes, however, we will have a sense of what is going on and how we can facilitate the healing grace God desires for us to have.

One of the best things we can do to bear up when we are struggling is to use the gift of memory. We have not always struggled; we have also known times of joy and peace. We have not always been spiritually dry; there have been times when we were spiritually wet. When we are struggling, remembering these times is beneficial. I have often asked people who were struggling to tell me about times when they were not. Always, they have been able to do so and taking the time to remember those moments is a positive experience in the midst of a negative one.

The common thread running through all of these means of enduring our struggles is the importance of remaining faithful. Our emotions cry out, "What's the use? It's not working. Give up. Quit." That's honest, but it is not helpful for a very simple reason: the only way to know when "God comes back" is to be there when it happens. We have to show up in the darkness if we are to see the light. We have to keep practicing the means of grace and other spiritual disciplines if they are ever to revive. We cannot tell how or when that will happen; we have to be present when it does. I do not mean "fake it to make it." That violates the honesty I wrote about earlier. I mean staying put and hanging on. In classic spiritual formation it is called making a vow of stability.

A primary component of this stability is community. I will write more extensively about this in chapter seven, but it needs to be noted here too. Stability includes continuing to be formed by a community, even when our own spiritual senses are dry, weak, and struggling. There is strength in community. For many, that will be community found in a local church, but I know some who have been so wounded by the church that even the thought of going to one somewhere is foreboding. So, let me be clear: I use community to mean any healthy group of people that keeps you from being alone.

I also mean "community" in terms of the tried-and-true, time-tested part of the Christian tradition in which you can find support and guidance.[13] Jonathan Wilson-Hartgrove remains in a local church community in Durham, North Carolina, but he is also deeply rooted in the Benedictine tradition, which affords benefits other than what he gets in one location.[14] I have several friends who are Oblates in the Order of St. Benedict, find nourishment in the Order of St. Luke, and engage in other expressions of communal life. As I write these words, I have added being an Affiliate Member of the Iona Community to my formation. I hope someday to make a pilgrimage there, but in the meantime, keeping the Rule of the Community and accessing other aspects of their common life online strengthens my life in Christ. No matter how we do it, remaining faithful—even when we don't feel like it—is necessary.

Finally, as we do things like this, we must remember that spiritual struggle is not a terminal disease. It will eventually pass. I have no idea when or how (about my own struggle and surely not about yours), but I know it will. There will again be "streams in the wilderness" (Isa 35:6). The rivers of living water will flow again. If my experience of this is like that of others, it will happen in ways and at times when we are not expecting it. We are often saved by surprise! That's why it is essential for us to keep on walking, even if we have to drag a leg as we walk for a while.

---

13. Jonathan Wilson-Hartgrove wrote a good book about this: *The Wisdom of Stability* (Paraclete Press, 2010).

14. See Jonathan Wilson-Hartgrove's *The Rule of Saint Benedict: A Contemporary Paraphrase* (Paraclete Press, 2012).

Chapter Five
The Design

When we moved to Nashville, we decided to build a house rather than purchase one. Our first step was deciding which model we wanted. The builder we chose offered a variety of homes from which to make our selection. Once we made the choice, however, everything followed the design for that particular house. It was not a cookie-cutter decision because there were options for us to consider before construction was completed and we moved in, but every choice we made was in relation to the design we selected.

Like our house in Nashville, life offers us a variety of choices about how we want to live. There is no one-size-fits-all lifestyle, and there are options within the basic choice we make, but we live in relation to the fundamental design we choose. In many respects our life revolves around the design we choose, and when it comes to matters of faith, the design of the Christian spiritual life is Christ. Paul reached the pinnacle of his desire for the Galatians when he wrote that he would not cease to labor on their behalf until Christ was formed in them (Gal 4:19). The essence of the Christian life is Christlikeness, an idea that I introduced in chapter one. We will now look at this idea in greater detail in this chapter.

In Romans, Paul wrote that God means for us to be conformed to Christ's image (Rom 8:29). That's the essence of Christlikeness, but before we go too far, we must ask, "Which Christ?" The Bible teaches there is the excarnate Christ and the incarnate Christ. The excarnate Christ is the second person of the Trinity, the Son of God. The excarnate Christ is often referred to as the cosmic Christ, the Christ who was with the Father from the beginning. The incarnate Christ is the person of Jesus, the Word made flesh (John 1:14), who lived on the earth for about thirty-three years. In traditional language, Jesus is referred to as the Son of Man, but more recently, the phrase is "the human one."[1] I like this phrasing, and as we will see, it is the incarnate Christ whom Paul had in mind when he exhorted the Galatians to become like Christ. Christ is the design for the spiritual life, and we see this in several significant ways.

First, Christ is the model of the spiritual life. As the human one, he revealed what the imago dei (Gen 1:26-28) was intended to look like before sin contaminated it. When the writer of Hebrews wrote that Jesus was like us in every way, except without sin, the author was not saying that Christ was above-and-beyond us, but rather that Christ was a picture of what humanity would have looked like if things had not gone wrong (Heb 4:15). If Christ was not the human one, then it makes no sense to describe the spiritual life as life in Christ. If Christ is like us in every respect save sin, however, then Christ's example is realistic. As the human

---

1. The *CEB Study Bible* has several excellent articles about referring to Jesus as the human one.

one, Christ lived the life that each one of us is meant to live. In Christ we see ourselves.

This means that the spiritual life is not an add-on to our life; it is the resurrection of the life that is already present in us because we are made in God's image. The spiritual life is intrinsic to our nature, not an invasion into it. The spiritual life is natural, not forced. The hunger for God is genuine because we are made in God's image, and made for God, and the incarnate Christ reveals this. Jesus himself showed that he, too, hungered for fellowship with the Father, often withdrawing to be alone with God (Luke 5:16). Jesus also said that his spiritual nourishment came from doing his Father's will (John 4:34); Jesus modeled every inclination for God that you and I have experienced.

When we examine the pattern of the incarnate Christ, we find it is a many-splendid thing. In chapter one, I described Jesus's life as the vision for our spiritual life. Now, we are ready to see a number of ways in which this is true.[2] We begin with Jesus's life as a prayer-filled life. We refer to this as the contemplative tradition. James Bryan Smith and Lynda Graybeal rightly note that "the central focus of Jesus's life was his relation with the Father."[3] From God's side, prayer is the revelation of God's heart toward us. From our side, prayer is our way of responding to God. It is no wonder that Jesus's disciples asked him to teach them to pray.

2. The Renovare spiritual formation ministry begun by Richard Foster gives us a great gift in describing the spiritual life in Christ-centered ways. The ministry's basic resource, *A Spiritual Formation Workbook* by James Bryan Smith (rev. ed. [HarperOne, 1999]), explores the life of Jesus in relation to our life. I have taught this pattern for years, and I make use of it in this chapter. I highly recommend the Renovare ministry.

3. Smith, *A Spiritual Formation Workbook*, 33.

They had seen the centrality of prayer in Jesus's life. Christ is our model for prayer.[4]

Christ also models the virtuous life. We call this the holiness tradition, and it was a model tested throughout Jesus's life. We see it first, immediately, after Jesus's baptism when the devil strongly tempted Jesus to give it all up before Jesus had hardly begun. Each of the three temptations was an assault on an aspect of Jesus's character. Henri Nouwen wrote of the three temptations as a temptation to be relevant, spectacular, and powerful, respectively.[5] To have succumbed to any one of the three would have been to compromise Jesus's ministry, but he rebuffed Satan's deception and continued with integrity to fulfill his life and ministry. The second wave of assaults on Jesus's virtue cannot be limited to one experience, or even a few. Almost from start to finish, the religious leaders tested Jesus, trying to trap him so that they could have evidence to condemn him. Time after time, however, Jesus eluded their grasp. Then, we see Jesus's final test in the Garden of Gethsemane when he suffered so much that his sweat was like "drops of blood" falling to the ground (Luke 22:44), yet Jesus ended up praying, "If it's not possible that this cup be taken away unless I drink it, then let it be what you want" (Matt 26:42).

Jesus's life and ministry were a testimony to virtue from start to finish. Today, we refer to this as holiness. The holy life is one rooted and centered in one's character, an integrity that Jesus described in the Beatitudes as purity of heart. Holiness is a life

---

4. It is also likely that the disciples requested this from Jesus because it was customary for a rabbi to give his pupils a common prayer. Jesus, of course, did this by providing what we call The Lord's Prayer, but we must also note that the disciples made their request on the heels of observing Jesus in prayer. It is impossible to separate Jesus's teaching about prayer from his practice of it.

5. Henri Nouwen, *In the Name of Jesus: Reflections on Christian Leadership* (Crossroad, 1989).

marked by love that is functional, healthy, and whole.[6] Jesus was holy in every way. He models the virtuous life.

Jesus's life was also Spirit-empowered. We describe this as the charismatic tradition. His birth was due to the Spirit's activity in Mary's life. At Jesus's baptism, the Holy Spirit descended upon him in the form of a dove. Immediately afterward, the Spirit sustained Jesus in the wilderness and enabled him to overcome Satan's temptations. When Jesus inaugurated his ministry in Nazareth, he said, "The Spirit of the Lord is upon me" (Luke 4:18). From that moment on, Jesus lived and ministered in the Spirit and before he ascended into heaven, Jesus promised that the Holy Spirit would come to strengthen and sustain us (Acts 1:8).

For every Christian, life in Christ is through the Holy Spirit's indwelling. The Holy Spirit is essential, and the Spirit is God active in and through us. We call this activity the fruit of the Spirit (Gal 5:22-23), which we will look at in more detail in chapter nine. For now, the point is to see that Jesus is our model for the Spirit-filled life.

Furthermore, Jesus models the compassionate life. We call this the social justice tradition. We sum it up in the word *compassion*. On several occasions the gospel writers note that Jesus was moved by compassion, but even without calling attention to it, we can see that compassion was the tone that ran throughout Jesus's life and ministry. Compassion includes sympathy and empathy, but it also goes beyond both. Compassion means that we identify with others so much that we take action for their betterment and on their behalf.

Compassion is the one-word description of the second great commandment: love your neighbor as yourself. As a Middle

6. Smith, *A Spiritual Formation Workbook*, 39.

Eastern sage, Jesus knew and embraced the idea of interbeing, which is what Jesus is describing in the second commandment. Interbeing is a depth of relationship with another person that eliminates the sense of separation. Interbeing is the recognition of our essential oneness with everyone and everything because we all come from the one source, who is God. Compassion springs from the awareness that every part of the creation is a precious work of God. Social justice is the way in which we seek to restore anyone and anything to their, and its, intended being. This is why forgiveness and healing marked Jesus's ministry; he is our model of compassion.

Additionally, Jesus lived a sacramental life. We call this the incarnational tradition. With respect to Christ's incarnation as Jesus we say, "the Word became flesh / and made his home among us" (John 1:14). This is the height of the sacramental life, but in Jesus's down-to-earth expression of such a life, Jesus revealed that God's presence is pervasive. Jesus's sacramental life included religious occasions and places, but was not limited to these. Jesus's sacramental life also showed God's comprehensive concern for life's totality. Jean Pierre de Caussade called this, "the sacrament of the present moment"; that is, living life in such a way that every moment is a God-moment.[7]

Jesus abandoned himself to this understanding of God's providence to such an extent that the word *interruption* never seemed to characterize the way he lived. Jesus stopped to bless children when the disciples thought he should be moving on; he stopped to restore a widow's son to life; he stopped yet again to restore a blind man's sight. When we read the gospels, we read about Jesus investing himself in life's ordinary events. He did this by living

---

7. Jean Pierre de Caussade, *Abandonment to Divine Providence.*

90 percent of his life as a carpenter in Nazareth. The sacramental life is one in which we affirm the sacredness of everyone, everything, and every moment. The goodness of the original creation has not been entirely lost; we see it present in life's little things. Jesus models the sacramental life.

Finally, Jesus lived a Word-centered life. We call this the evangelical tradition.[8] As the Word made flesh, Jesus manifested the root meaning of *evangelical*: one who lives good news. I agree with Henri Nouwen's claim that Jesus is the Gospel.[9] The Gospel is a person, not a principle. The relationship that the Gospel produces is an I-Thou relationship, a person-to-person and heart-to-heart relationship with God, not a doctrine-based, belief-oriented (and evaluated) relationship.

In Jesus we see that the *Word* is not only a spoken word or a written word but it is also, and ultimately, a lived word. This is what the world is crying out for today—a Christianity that *looks* like Christ, not just one that speaks and writes about him. The world is hungering for the Word to be made flesh again (and again) through the lives of those who profess to be Jesus's disciples. To say that Jesus modeled the Word-centered life means that he lived it. In fact, his authority was different from many of the religious leaders of his day precisely because his life was a lived theology, an enacted faith. Jesus models the Word-centered life.

These dimensions of Jesus's life are not only the model of the spiritual life, but also they lead us into the second feature of Jesus's

8. Sadly, in our day, the Evangelical tradition has been hijacked by fundamentalism and nationalism, but it in its historic sense, the Evangelical tradition remains among the key streams of the Christian faith.
9. Henri Nouwen, *Jesus, A Gospel* (Orbis Books, 2001).

pattern.[10] His life is the message of the spiritual life. There is an old saying: "I'd rather see a sermon than hear one any day." This exactly what Jesus did: he personified the proclamation. He lived the theology. He summed it up in one sentence: "Love each other just as I have loved you" (John 15:12). Here is the perfect combination of information and incarnation. The first half of what he said had already been said, all the way back in Leviticus 19:18. Indeed, the first half of Jesus's sentence is the second great commandment, and it's in the second half of what he said that we see the personification of the message, "*as I have loved you.*"

So, what kind of love did Jesus exhibit? The answer can be stated in three words: love for all. He demonstrated his love in conventional ways to the people whom we would assume to be the objects of Jesus's love. So that no one missed the comprehensiveness of his love, however, Jesus offered it to those who had been marginalized, judged, and condemned. He offered it to Gentiles and to Samaritans. He even offered it to law-breakers. Jesus offered his love again and again, to everyone.

In doing so, Jesus incarnated the message he had given in his Sermon on the Mount: "Just as your heavenly Father is complete in showing love to everyone, so also you must be complete" (Matt 5:48). The world already had incomplete love. Religion already had incomplete love. Jesus referred to this incompleteness in the two verses before Matthew 5:48. Incomplete love is loving only those who love you and showing regard for only those who give you respect. Jesus said that kind of love is nothing to brag about, much less a definition of love. In short, Jesus said that love is not

10. Renovaré has produced an excellent anthology and workbook (*Devotional Classics* [HarperOne, 1993]) that takes users deeper into the five streams of the Christlike life. Using this resource provides the opportunity to delve into the heart of fifty-two authors and their classic works.

love until it is shown to everyone. Richard Rohr restates what Jesus said, "Either you love everything or there is reason to doubt that you love anything."[11]

We can see that Jesus's message of love made it into the early church. Writing about fifty years later, St. John said, "Little children, let's not love with words or speech but with action and truth" (1 John 3:18). That's it! Love with skin on it. Love enfleshed. Love complete. Love for all. To speak of Jesus's message of love in any other way is to misrepresent it. To commend the spiritual life as life in Christ with any other interpretation of love is bogus. All means all.

It's a tall order, one that none can accomplish alone, which brings us to the third dimension of Christ's pattern. Jesus is the means through whom we live the spiritual life. Without this, Jesus's model and message is a dead-end spirituality. With Christ as the means, however, the spiritual life is attractive and attainable. Jesus was referring to himself as the means of the spiritual life when he said, "I am the vine; you are the branches. If you remain in me and I in you, then you will produce much fruit" (John 15:5). Abiding in Jesus is the means by which the fruit of the Spirit comes alive in and through us. The spiritual life is a derivative of Jesus's life in us. Referring to his resurrection, he told his disciples plainly, "Because I live, you will live too" (John 14:19).

Jesus is the pattern: the model, the message, and the means. By re-centering the Galatians in Christ rather than in the law, Paul aimed to move the Galatians back into life and away from legalism. The relationship is always I-Thou, not I-It. Dr. Dennis Kinlaw wrote about this same thing: "That is what Christianity

---

11. Richard Rohr, "The Great Chain of Being," in *The Mendicant* newsletter from the Center for Action and Contemplation, Summer 2019, vol. 9. no. 3.

has to offer the world, a personal relationship with God."[12] Moving beyond the juridical metaphor of the courtroom (from which our theology of justification is derived), Dr. Kinlaw emphasizes the metaphors of friendship, family, marriage, indwelling, and identity as the primary ways of understanding our life in Christ.

With respect to identity, Dr. Kinlaw wrote that he came to see this metaphor later than others. He discovered the metaphor of identity in Jesus's words, "Those who receive you are also receiving me, and those who receive me are receiving the one who sent me" (Matt 10:40). Dr. Kinlaw writes that this is the deepest metaphor of all: "Sure, Christ is life for me. But this also means that I am to be Christ to other people." If Jesus had not said this level of oneness between him and us is possible, then it would be preposterous even to mention it. Just like a vine and a branch, however, it is impossible to tell exactly where the vine stops and the branch starts. The connection is so natural that the two entities blend together. This is what Paul meant when he wrote, "For to me, living is Christ" (Phil 1:21 NRSV)—that is, there comes a point of union between our spirit and the Spirit of the risen Christ when it is pointless to ask, "Is this me or Jesus?" It just IS.

Before we write this off as a kind of spirituality that is so rare that it hardly exists, I would point out that it is the kind of life together that couples attain after living together for years. Jeannie and I have been married for over fifty years, and we really do have a common mind. We think each other's thoughts and speak each other's words. A common life has taken shape over the decades. Far from being strange, it is sacred. Far from being weird, it is wonderful. In fact, it is a life together that we would not change for any other way of relating.

---

12. Dennis Kinlaw, *We Live as Christ* (Francis Asbury Press, 2001), 16.

Paul wanted the Galatians to have Christ formed in them because we live as Christ. Christ is our life. Christ is the model, message, and means for our lives. We live by Christ, to Christ, with Christ, in Christ, like Christ, and for Christ.[13] This is what the essence, experience, and expression of the spiritual life is all about.

---

13. As you like, go back to chapter one and review these six dimensions.

Chapter Six
The Process

O ur children's prenatal development was a time of vigil and joy. Jeannie's regular obstetric visits provided us with updates that only intensified our expectations, and when John and Katrina were each born, the growth each had experienced in the womb continued as each moved forward in life. We monitored their growth with lists and charts in their baby books, discovered goals, and celebrated achievements for various ages. Our joy only increased as we watched them develop. Now, they are middle-aged, and we continue to rejoice as we see them grow.

Comparisons with human development are appropriate as we explore the process of our spiritual formation. Apparently, Paul thought this as well because he used the labor-pain analogy in his writing. Paul's desire for the Galatians to have Christ formed is captured by using the analogy of human development. He did not, however, invent the analogy. We also see it in Jesus's original invitation to his disciples: "Follow me and I will make you fish for people" (Mark 1:17 NRSV). The English translation obscures the developmental nature of his invitation. Consider the original

Greek: "Follow me and I will make you **to become** fishers of people" (bold font mine). Jesus's intention to *make* them disciples carried with it his invitation for them *to become* such. As we follow them through the rest of the New Testament, we see that they were always becoming; they were continuing to grow in the grace and knowledge of Christ (2 Pet 3:18).

Our life in Christ is one of ongoing development. There is no other way to look at it. When you think about it, how could it be otherwise? We are living in relation to God, who is eternal and infinite. We can never come to the end of that. Yet we have substituted a variety of "arrival" programs for assessing our formation and maturity. We have devised a host of litmus tests for determining who is ahead of whom in the spiritual life. If nothing else, I am writing this chapter to put an end to that way of thinking and to invite you to realize that Jesus's invitation to embark on a journey is an invitation to a never-ending journey.[1]

There's no doubt that Paul had this understanding of the spiritual life, and it comes through clearly elsewhere in his letters. Paul prayed that the Ephesians would be "filled entirely with the fullness of God" (Eph 3:19). A little later in the same letter, he urged them to be "fully grown, measured by the standard of the fullness of Christ" (Eph 4:13). Taken out of context, this kind of thinking is absurd and dangerous, and could lead to hubris, arrogance, and spiritual megalomania. When Paul's words remain connected to God's eternal nature and Christ's universality, however, they become incentives never to quit. Paul's words incentivize us to realize that, no matter how spiritually mature we become, we can

---

1. Robert Mulholland wrote *Invitation to a Journey* (InterVarsity Press, 1993) as a winsome overview into the experience of spiritual formation. A little over ten years later, he wrote a second book, *The Deeper Journey* (InterVarsity, 2006), in which he shows that our journey into Christ is one that never ends.

always take one more step in faith. We never arrive. The process of spiritual formation is ongoing and, as such, our life in Christ has some identifiable and important qualities.

First, being formed in Christ provides us with a realistic understanding of the spiritual life. E. Stanley Jones described his own formation this way: "Every stage of being is a stage of becoming. It is open-ended.... To commune with God and to grow forever in his likeness—yes, but never to arrive—is a possible and perfect fulfillment of my being as a finite person."[2] He often referred to himself as "a Christian under construction," and when people asked him to name the best years of his life, he usually replied, "the next ten." Here is a realistic understanding of the spiritual life. It combines the joy of living in Christ in the present moment with the anticipation of living more fully in Christ in the future.

This realism was missing in the life of the man who Jesus said owned land that produced a harvest bigger than his barns could hold. In his abundance, he very naturally decided to tear down his existing barns and build bigger ones to hold everything. So far, so good. Then, however, the man made the mistake of a lifetime, saying to himself, "You have stored up plenty of goods, enough for several years. Take it easy! Eat, drink and enjoy yourself" (Luke 12:19). The reality of his abundance made him proud. It stopped the natural planting, tending, and harvesting processes and put him in neutral. He felt he had arrived; he told himself that he had enough. Jesus ended this parable saying that God called the man a fool. Spiritual foolishness is thinking we have all we need. Life

2. E. Stanley Jones, *A Song of Ascents* (Abingdon Press, 1968). Jones considered this to be his spiritual autobiography, and he wrote it when he was eighty-four. He clearly recognized the never-ending nature of the spiritual journey.

in Christ is realizing that no matter where we are, there is always something more.

Such realism not only keeps us in motion, but also it keeps us humble. In fact, against the backdrop of God's eternality, it is pointless to compare ourselves with others and it is even worse to believe we have all we need. Against the backdrop of eternity there is no difference between the person who has been a Christian for thirty years and the one who has been so for thirty minutes. It is foolish and wrong for anyone to view themselves as ahead or behind another. We are all one in Christ Jesus (Gal 3:28). To be formed in Christ is to be formed realistically.

Second, to be formed in Christ is also to be given a practical program for growing spiritually. Paul described the program to Timothy by saying, "Train yourself for a holy life" (1 Tim 4:7). In this phase we follow the process from the birthing room to the gym. With a realistic understanding of spiritual life, we can exercise our will to grow, knowing we will do so in the right ways and in good directions. It is the phase Paul described as carrying out (completing) our salvation with reverence and devotion (Phil 2:12). The reverence comes from the realism we have previously described; the devotion comes from recognizing that (as Oswald Chambers put it) we must work out what God has worked in.[3]

Reverence prevents us from ascribing our salvation to anything other than grace, and devotion prevents us from becoming passive with respect to our formation. Keeping reverence and devotion linked together forms the life of Christ in us. There is no one-size-fits-all formula for the spiritual life, but there is a universal principle: grace + response = growth. God does not bypass

---

3. Oswald Chambers, *My Utmost for His Highest*, June 6. This devotional classic is available in a host of formats and from a variety of publishers.

our wills; God engages them. We are co-creators with God in the formative process.

Life in Christ also has a formational pace. Like everything else, it is a pace of grace. Some of us need to hear this because we are temperamentally disposed to "put the pedal to the metal" when we enter a new experience. The temptation to do this increases if we become Christians later in life and feel that we must make up for lost time. Let us be clear, however, of this one thing: freneticism is not a manifestation of faith. More precisely, freneticism is what Eugene Peterson called, "a long obedience in the same direction."[4] The Bible even reminds us that it is those who *endure to the end* that are saved (Matt 24:13). We are formed into Christ in a little-by-little fashion.

The curriculum for this formative program is what we typically call the spiritual disciplines, and what John Wesley referred to as the means of grace. For quite a while I thought of these disciplines as spiritual practices, which they are. Over time, however, I have come to see them as much more. I agree with Ruth Haley Barton that the disciplines are the means by which we arrange our lives for transformation.[5] Decades before she wrote about the disciplines this way, William Temple expressed a similar view, that the spiritual practices are "the bringing of the inner life under the control of the Holy Spirit by the perpetual discipline which brings us back, day by day, to the remembrance and companionship of Jesus."[6] Along the same line of thought, Joan Chittister commented that the Rule of Benedict (itself a document of

---

4. Eugene Peterson, *A Long Obedience in the Same Direction*, 2nd ed. (InterVarsity Press, 2000).

5. Ruth Haley Barton, *Sacred Rhythms* (InterVarsity Press, 2006).

6. William Temple, *Christian Faith and Life* (SCM Press, 1957), 101.

spiritual practices) is "not a set of daily activities; it's a way of life, an attitude of mind, an orientation of soul."[7]

If it seems that I am belaboring this point, you are correct. My reason for doing so is to liberate the spiritual disciplines from being essentially understood as actions to being understood as the way our attitudes are formed into Christlikeness. The spiritual disciplines are essentially the patterning of our inner and outer life (individually and collectively), so that we are disposed toward holiness of heart and life.[8] In this book, I use the Wesleyan view to describe the disciplines: works of piety and works of mercy, the instituted and prudential means of grace.[9]

There are five Wesleyan instituted means of grace, which are also referred to as works of piety: prayer, searching the scripture, the Lord's Supper, fasting, and Christian conferencing. These disciplines are essentially (but not exclusively) intended to shape our inward lives into Christlikeness. Prayer is our means of communion with God. Searching the scripture (not simply reading the Bible) is the practice of *lectio divina* so that the written words in scripture become the living word of God in our lives. The Lord's Supper is the Eucharist, receiving God's grace and offering ourselves to God as instruments of peace. Fasting is the deliberate withholding of something (not just food) so that literal and figurative space can be made for a more concentrated attentiveness

7. Joan Chittister, *The Rule of Benedict* (Crossroad, 1992), 30.
8. Richard Foster's book, *Celebration of Discipline, 40th anniversary edition* (HarperOne, 2018), is an excellent place to explore the spiritual disciplines. The Renovaré ministry's anthology and workbook, *Spiritual Classics* (HarperOne, 2000), enables users to explore Foster's inward, outward, and corporate disciplines through fifty-two devotional classics. These two volumes are unsurpassable as an introduction to the disciplines.
9. Elaine Heath's book, *Five Means of Grace* (Abingdon Press, 2017), is an excellent overview of the instituted means of grace. I also wrote on the means of grace in *Devotional Life in the Wesleyan Tradition: A Workbook* (Upper Room Books, 1995).

on God. Finally, Christian conferencing is gathering together with other Christians for edification and accountability. By these means we incline our hearts to the Lord (Josh 24:23); through these disciplines we cultivate personal holiness.

The prudential means of grace, often called works of piety, include: doing no harm, doing good, and participating in the public services where faith is formed. Doing no harm means that no Christian knowingly hurts another person, whether in word or deed. Doing no harm is the elimination of negative energy in our lives and the destructive ways in which that energy manifests itself. Doing good is the inflowing of positive energy through any and all means to edify and enrich others. Finally, participating in public services where faith is formed is what John Wesley called "attending the ordinances of God," which was his way of extending our individual practice of the disciplines (works of piety) into corporate expressions.[10]

The corporate expressions pertain to worshipping God in the Church, and to participating in ecclesial and civic groups where there are opportunities to grow and express our faith. In the Wesleyan tradition, one of the meaningful expressions of this life together is in the annual Covenant Renewal Service.[11] Wesley, like others before and after him, believed that Christians need to keep their commitments current. So, each year (usually on December 31) the Methodists gather to renew their faith in God. However it is done, the prudential means of grace form us in Christlike life together and they dispose our hearts toward the world, creating within us the spirit of servanthood. They cultivate social holiness.

---

10. Rueben Job's book, *Three Simple Rules* (Abingdon Press, 2007), is an excellent rendition of the three prudential means of grace with respect to how we can live them today.

11. Magrey deVega wrote about this in *One Faithful Promise* (Abingdon Press, 2016).

Before we leave the disciplines, it is important once again to emphasize that their purpose is to form us into the character of Christ, both inwardly and outwardly. John Wesley wrote about this in his treatise "The Character of a Methodist" (1742). In so many words he said that any and all spiritual practices fall short of their goal if we see them as ends in themselves. They are *means* of grace; they are practices aimed at the target of Christlikeness. For Wesley and, indeed for all Christians, that aim is character formation. Wesley described such character formation as having five phrases: loving God, rejoicing in God, giving thanks to God, praying continually, and loving others.[12] The last two descriptions of our character formation link the instituted and prudential means of grace, making them parts of the larger whole, which is what we call life in Christ. With the disciplines, we have our curriculum for being inwardly and outwardly alive in Christ.

Third, the formative process is also a way of guarding our hearts. We see this in the experience of the Galatians themselves, who had turned back to living in the flesh. The temptation was not unique to the Galatians; Paul observed it in himself and in other congregations. It is a temptation that every generation of Christians since then has faced. Howard Baker comments on this reversal when he wrote, "Having been forgiven, given the Spirit, and baptized, we think we are now capable of living this life by our own independent efforts...and as a result our spiritual formation is arrested."[13]

We fall prey to this reversal through good intentions. We can naturally express our gratitude to God by "doing all we can" to live our faith. Out of a spirit of thanksgiving we can turn a

---

12. I wrote about this in *Five Marks of a Methodist* (Abingdon Press, 2015).
13. Howard Baker, *The Life with God Bible* (HarperOne, 2005), 324 nt.

grace-based experience into a performance-oriented enterprise. Rejoicing in God's goodness toward us, we can easily say, "Thank you, God, for everything you have done for me and in me; I can take it from here." Here's the thing: when we say this, there is a raft of options for regaining control. The number of groups, each with its own litmus test for faithfulness, is beyond number.

One of the most radical things we can do in our spiritual formation is never sell our soul to any "company store." The moment we do that, the group has us, not God. Or to say it another way, we will begin to take our cues from the group rather than from God. Unhealthy groups will never resist our dependency; in fact, they thrive on it. Left unchecked, faithfulness to God becomes synonymous with faithfulness to the group. That's exactly what the Judaisers were doing to the Galatians. It was as if they were saying, "The genuineness of your faith is in relation to your faithfulness to us."

Life in Christ, however, is a matter of the heart, not of the group. That's why Solomon wrote long ago, "Above all else, guard your heart, for it is the wellspring of life" (Prov 4:23 NIV). The image that Solomon had in mind was that of the watchman on the city walls. The watchman's express purpose was ensuring that no enemy slipped up and slipped in to overthrow the town. Watchmen were on duty throughout the day and night (continuously), and they kept watch in all directions (comprehensively). No time of the day was exempt; no part of life was ignored. Paul came along and said essentially the same thing to Timothy: "Focus on working on your own development and on what you teach" (1 Tim 4:16). And the last time Paul met with the Ephesian elders, he exhorted them, "Watch yourselves..." (Acts 20:28).

No matter how long or how far we go in our faith, we must never hand over the control of our souls to others.

This is not selfishness, it is survival. Unscrupulous people are always waiting to subjugate us to themselves, in both overt and covert ways. Guarding our hearts does not mean we become independent operators, separated from or unconcerned about our faith in relation to the Christian tradition. In fact, the opposite turns out to be the case. If we remain rooted in the larger Christian tradition, we will more readily remain immune from the captivity of a particular group, for we will always recognize that the faith is larger than any one group's interpretation of it. The Judaisers wanted the Galatians to rejoin their club. Paul essentially said, "Don't do it! You belong to God, not to them."

When E. Stanley Jones arrived in India in 1907 to begin his service as a Methodist missionary, he was not there long before he saw a problem: many Indians were interested in Jesus, but not in the Church. It did not take him long to recognize what was going on, that the Church had become so institutionalized that it looked like the state (i.e., Great Britain) or like a denomination (e.g., Methodism). Many Indian people said to him, "We want Christ but not the Church." He knew he had a decision to make: whether to fall into the pattern of being a conventional missionary (who blended Christ and the Church into an unappealing combination) or to go the unconventional way and separate the individual (Jesus) from the institution.

Jones chose the unconventional way, writing that "Christianity must be defined as Christ, not the Old Testament, not Western civilization, not even the system built around him in the West, but Christ himself and to be a Christian is to follow him."[14] His Christ-emphasis opened doors into non-Christian settings but, ironically, it also closed doors in some Christian circles. Institutional church leaders and some fellow missionaries did not know how to relate to him as he went around preaching that the Indian people could become Christians without having to buy into all the institutional trappings surrounding Jesus.

To be formed into Christ is a radical experience. It challenges us at the deepest level of our being. It will challenge those who believe that the validity of a person's faith hinges on whether the group agrees. As we will see in chapter eight, however, the process of being formed into Christ is the most liberating experience we will ever know. It is the experience that Paul yearned for the Galatians to have. It is the experience that God, through the Holy Spirit, wants us to have as well.

---

14. E. Stanley Jones, *The Christ of the Indian Road* (Abingdon Press, 1925), 26. Jones's list is in relation to the three major ways conventional missionaries were trying to commend Christ to the Indian people. Jones saw that, not only were those ways not working, but also they were widening the gap further. I am convinced that Jones's early experience in India explains why, for the rest of his life, Jones kept the spotlight on Christ.

Chapter Seven
The Environment

I graduated from college with a double major in sociology and religion. I have always been glad about this. The combination has provided a balance and breadth to my life through the interaction of the two academic disciplines. One of the things the two disciplines remind me of is that the environment in which we are spiritually formed is as important as the content of our formation. I see this same perspective in Paul's letter to the Galatians when he writes that he longs for Christ to be formed "in you" (4:19). As we have shown, Christ is the content of the spiritual life; "in you" is the environment.

Jesus expressed the same view when he taught about wine and wineskins (Matt 9:17). The wine is the content, but it must have a good container holding it. In the same way, our life in Christ is shaped and sustained by the environment in which we are formed. In Paul's two words, *in you*, we have the opportunity to explore the twofold setting in which our formation occurs. The first reading of *in you* leads us to think about the personal environment of our formation. A closer look, however, reveals that the word *you* in the original Greek is plural, which gives us the opportunity to explore the role of community in our formation.

We begin with the personal environment. Even though, here, the Greek uses the plural form of *you*, there is no doubt that Paul also had our personal formation in mind. In 1 Corinthians 12:27, Paul wrote, "Now you are the body of Christ and individually members of it" (NRSV). With these words, he showed the interplay between the individual and communal aspects of our faith. We begin with the personal environment because it is what we bring with us into our community. In our communal environment we are reminded that we live in Christ in a setting larger than our own experience, but neither do we live in that larger setting without bringing our experience to it.

E. Stanley Jones emphasized this as he taught about the God's kingdom (the largest expression of the communal environment), writing that we must bring the best self that we can into the community. In fact, he named bringing a deformed self into Christian community as the second enemy to abundant living.[1] He wrote that the first enemy of the spiritual life is a lack of faith in someone or something beyond ourselves, and then with that lack, a deformed (egocentric) self fills the void: "When God is no longer the center, we become the center."[2] It is not a lifegiving center, however, as Paul wrote to the Romans: "If you live on the basis of selfishness, you are going to die" (Rom 8:13).

---

1. E. Stanley Jones, *Abundant Living* (Whitmore and Stone, 1942), which is now reprinted by Abingdon Press in both paperback and e-book editions. In the book, Jones focuses for a week (Week 7) on the self but weaves the self throughout other parts of the book as well. He also wrote about egocentricity in many of his other books.

2. Jones, *Abundant Living*, Week 7, Sunday.

A deformed (egocentric) self becomes the environment for a deformed spirituality. It's what Paul called "living in the flesh" in his letter to the Galatians. It is what the Bible describes as idolatry— when any person, place, or thing other than God occupies center stage. Thomas Merton exposed the same truth, writing about the false self.[3] In our day, James Finley and Richard Rohr have provided valuable insights into the peril of the false self and the importance of living as the true selves (i.e., imago dei) God made us to be.[4] We explored the false self/true self phenomenon in chapter two; I only bring it up again here to show that the quality of our spiritual life that we bring into community largely depends on whether or not we have experienced the movement from the false self to the true self. Assuming that we have, we can turn our attention to looking at some of the gifts that the true self gives us in the environment of our formation.

First, we bring a unique self into the community. We share the imago dei as human beings, but we bear the imago dei in un-repeatable, individual ways. Howard Baker puts it this way: "The Christ-in-us-life is a one-of-a-kind story."[5] Just as we have unique fingerprints, so we also have an unrepeated soul print. God is a creator, not a cloner. The importance of this cannot be overstated because entering into community has the power to pull us away from our uniqueness and into more generic expressions. On the positive side, we call this act of joining community having shared faith with others; on the negative side, however, it can lead to the

---

3. Thomas Merton, *New Seeds of Contemplation* (New Directions, 1961), multiple meditations.

4. James Finley, *Merton's Palace of Nowhere: A Search for God Through Awareness of the True Self* (Ave Maria Press, 1978). Richard Rohr, *Falling Upward* (Jossey-Bass, 2011) and *Immortal Diamond* (Jossey-Bass, 2013).

5. *The Life with God Bible* (Zondervan, 2009), 325.

kind of "group think" that we exposed in the last chapter. In other words, it is necessary to bring a healthy and strong sense of self into community, lest it be lost in the communal environment.

Second, we bring a contributive self into community. Because no one is living our story, everyone can learn something, or benefit, from our story. One of the primary ways this occurs is through using the gifts of the Spirit. These gifts are described in several places in the Bible (Rom 12:6-8; 1 Cor 12; Eph 4:7-11), but Paul made it clear that no one has all the gifts, and that the gifts are distributed through the Holy Spirit's work in our lives (1 Cor 12:1-11). We have different gifts, the gifts have different expressions, and they produce different results (1 Cor 12:4-6).[6] This means that we come into community filled and equipped by the Spirit to make a unique contribution to it.

It is impossible to examine the gifts of the Spirit in detail, but because they have been misunderstood and misused in various ways, several considerations are appropriate to include in this book.[7] The first is that the gifts are not to be hierarchicalized. No gift is more important than another. This is likely the way that the gifts of the Spirit have been most abused—by using them to allege that one Christian is better than another. This is not the case! We remember this as we recall that we are individual members of the body of Christ. One part cannot say another part is unneeded (1 Cor 12:15-26) any more than our neurological system can claim independence from our cardio-pulmonary system. The gifts of the Spirit operate in a symbiotic relationship. When they

---

6. The three words—*gifts, ministries, activities*—reveal the proliferation of individuation that's possible through the gifts of the Spirit.

7. If you want to study the gifts of the spirit in more detail, I recommend going to umc.org, and then using the search feature and typing in: "Exploring Your Spiritual Gifts."

become competitive, the spiritual life (individually and collectively) suffers.

Another thing to note about the gifts of the Spirit is that some to be permanent in us, while others may be temporary. This reality reflects again the Spirit's sovereignty in giving them to us in the first place. My personal belief is that we should view all the gifts as temporary (at least in their specific expressions); if one or more appear to be permanent that is because the Spirit chooses to continue to use us in that way repeatedly. The problem with viewing any gift as permanent is that it can become something that we think we possess and control. By holding our gifts loosely, we leave their duration up to God. We exercise them with humility.

Third, it is important to recognize that our gifts almost always interact with the gifts of others. We are not independent operators. The spiritual gifts are not meant to make us stand out, but to help us blend in. We use our gifts best when a larger need, opportunity, or ministry draws us into using the gift. In fact, one of the best ways to know what gifts you may have is paying attention to those times when you say, "Someone ought to be doing something about that," or when you learn about a particular ministry and you think to yourself, "I would like to be involved in that." God makes us in ways that fit into God's mission. We will explore this idea in more detail in chapter nine.

Finally, we exercise our spiritual gifts in the context of liberty. Some people never identify and make use of their gifts because they are afraid that they might claim a gift that they do not have. The important thing to understand is that it is not our task to be certain we have a gift, but only committed to using whatever gifts we do have. If we set out to use a particular gift, only to discover later that we do not have that gift, there's no harm, no foul. We learn by doing, not by having to "get it right" before we do take action. For decades, I have told students, "If you head out on the holiness highway and discover you're going in the wrong direction, you can always make a U-turn." So, if you think you have (or may have) a particular gift of the Spirit, go to work along that line. Reality will either confirm your discernment or give you another opportunity to try something else.

All of this happens in the context of the seasons of the spiritual life. We looked at those seasons in chapter two. I mention them again only to show that, as we move through the ages and stages of our lives, we will alter the ways in which we use our gifts. God takes our lives seriously, and so must we. We will not be using our gifts at age seventy the way we did when we were thirty. The gifts that are more permanent in nature will be used differently. We may find that new gifts will be given to us by the Spirit, who wants to use us in ways that we had not been used before. Whatever the case, we will develop our life in Christ with a spirit of confidence ("God is not finished with me yet") and peace ("I cannot do everything, but I can do something") that will keep us meaningfully engaged.

Looking at our individual environment as a whole, it is in the dimension of our spiritual formation where we deepen and widen our sense of communion with God. Our individual growth results in becoming more contemplative, it is not a solely interior experience or one that is isolated from our actions. Rather, it is more about our response to Jesus's invitation for us to enter our rooms, shut our doors, and pray to our heavenly Father (Matt 6:6). It is in this sacred place (where our human spirit interacts with the Holy Spirit) that we sharpen our skills of listening and

responding.[8] When we are formed inwardly with these disposi-
tions alive within us, then we are ready to enter into the second
formative environment: the communal environment.

Life in Christ is life together. Dietrich Bonhoeffer described
such a life by writing that we "meet one another as bringers of the
message of salvation."[9] This is a beautiful and powerful way to connect the personal environment with the communal environment.
In *Life Together*, Bonhoeffer described the community he formed
in Finkenwalde, a community that incarnated the individual and
communal dimensions of formation in what he referred to as time
alone, time with others, and time for ministry. It was also a community in which confession and holy communion were frequent
and influential. The model Dietrich Bonhoeffer provides us in his
book is replicable for us today.

The importance of the communal environment cannot be
overstated. We are living in a time of individualism—an odd
time in which people yearn for relationships but live isolated lives
within their electronic devices. With respect to the spiritual life,
the result is a privatized spirituality that bears little resemblance
(or at least a diminished likeness) to what life in Christ is meant to
be. Once again, if we keep the metaphor of the body of Christ in
mind, then we see the impossibility of one system being separated
from another. In fact, a single system only makes sense (and sur-
vives) when it interacts with other systems. That's why Paul wrote
that one part of the body of Christ cannot say to another, "I don't
need you" (1 Cor 12:15-26). No, indeed! The fact is that we need

8. John Mogabgab notes these two things in his excellent book, *Communion,
Community, Commonweal* (Upper Room Books, 1995), 18. One of the blessings of
my life was to know John and receive the many blessings his friendship bestowed.

9. Dietrich Bonhoeffer, *Life Together* (Harper & Row, 1954), 23.

each other, and the communal environment enriches what was begun in the cave of the heart.

As with our individual environment, the communal experience is larger than we can write about in this book. There are four important formative experiences in community, however, that I want to mention here: remembering, celebrating, communicating, and guiding.[10] With respect to remembering, I mean everything we typically associate with Christian education. The word *disciple* means *learner*. One of the roles of Christian community is continuing to help us take what we know and expand that knowledge. When we gather in community, we come together to grow in the grace and knowledge of Jesus Christ (2 Pet 3:18). Life in Christ has an educational dimension. Here, I mean more than intellectual maturation; I mean that, in community, we re-member. In community, we gather to remind ourselves what matters most to us and to recommit ourselves to those things. It is easy to get strung out during the week, becoming "five miles wide and a half-inch deep." Remembering is the recurring act of re-centering ourselves and re-presenting ourselves as living sacrifices to God (Rom 12:1).

This kind of growing flows easily into celebration. As we gather to recall what we most deeply believe and give ourselves anew to it, we experience a revival of joy. We do this through the various ways that community invites us to praise. Vertically, we offer our praise to God; horizontally, we praise the sacredness of others and the goodness of God's creation. The two dimensions come together for us in the moments of celebration afforded to

---

10. I am deliberately choosing the four experiences that John Mogabgab highlighted in his book, *Communion, Community, Commonweal.* I have awaited a place in my writing to honor and memorialize John. Here is my opportunity to do so.

us in community, especially when we celebrate the Lord's Supper. The eucharistic liturgy invites us to give thanks, not just in terms of the wine and the bread, but also as a whole-life celebration of all that it means to be alive in Christ. This celebration may be through expressions of general thanksgiving, but they also almost always include specific things for which we are grateful. Community strikes in us the note of joy.

Thirdly, we discover communication in community. This, of course, includes the teaching and preaching that we experience. It includes the music and other audio-visual opportunities to connect with the message. In this book, however, I am thinking about the ways we communicate with each other when we come together in Jesus's name when our faith is shared through conversation, group discussion, formal instruction, proclamation, and so on. Communication arises from the communion we experience with others in these various settings. In a broad way, it is what Paul called "speaking the truth with love" (Eph 4:15). Community provides many ways for this to happen.

Finally, community guides us. As with the other three experiences, guidance comes through a variety of media and methods, but the end result is coming to know God's will (afresh or in an entirely new way) and finding in community the encouragement to do that will. In community we are guided into a greater awareness of, and appreciation for, living in God's kingdom. We are encouraged to use our lives as instruments of God's peace, and guidance includes opportunities for discernment, support, and implementation. But it also affords a place to come to when our actions are resisted, or when we fail to carry out our actions as we had intended. Guidance in community is multi-faceted: finding the path, walking the path, and getting back on the path when we veer off course.

Putting it all together, we find that the communal environment creates the sense of oneness between and among us. In community we embody the truth that we are all one in Christ Jesus (Gal 3:28). This is neither a formal relationship nor a static state; it is a oneness that leads to one-anothering (e.g., John 15:12 and 1 John 4:11). In community we rejoice with those who rejoice, and we weep with those who weep (Rom 12:15). Compassion is a hallmark of community.

These are some of the characteristics of the environment where life in Christ begins, continues, and ends. There may have been a time when I could have ended the chapter at this point, but we are not living in such a time. Despite the picture we have painted of the formative environment, we are living in a time when a growing number of people are not affiliating with religion in general, or the church in particular. Additionally, a growing number of people are also leaving organized religion and the church. There is an identifiable and increasing group today referred to as the "Nones and Dones." It is impossible to write about the environment for cultivating life in Christ without addressing this reality.

The fact is, both religion and the church have too often failed to provide the kind of environment we have examined in this chapter. It may be that you are one of those whose hopes for religion and the church have been dealt a blow by the very people who claim to know God and to follow Jesus. You may already be on the outside, looking in. Or, like many others, you may be a "done," but you are still hanging around on the periphery of religious belief and the institutional church. If you are such a person,

I wish we could go over the rest of this chapter together. But since that's not possible, I will do the best I can to speak honestly about the dilemma we find ourselves in today.

More than anything else, I want you to know that I (and many others) understand there are valid reasons why the attraction to religion and to the church has declined. There is no need to go into detail about this. You have your reasons, and I want you to know that I accept them, and I lament that conditions have been such that you have moved to the margins of either formal religion or the institutional church. Too often, the kind of environment I have described in this chapter is lacking or missing. The truth is, you are perceptive and correct to notice its absence, and decide not to put yourself into a deformative or toxic community. It is impossible for me to ask you to return, because I do not know specifically why you left (or never came through the door to begin with), and I have no idea what options may be near you for finding a formative environment.

I do believe, however, that the implosion of both religion and the church in our day is necessary, and that it is a prelude to a resurrection of both.[11] My encouragement for you not to give up entirely is based on that vision of resurrection, a kind of "you ain't seen nothin' yet" hope for the future. This in no way justifies or assuages any pain you have experienced; it only means that the pain is not the final word. So, I offer my take on two questions related to the situation we find ourselves in today.

---

11. Diana Butler Bass, *Christianity After Religion: The End of the Church and the Birth of a New Spiritual Awakening* (HarperOne, 2012). Bass writes in detail about the passage from death to life that takes place with respect to religion and the church. She also offers that passage as a sign of hope. In a similar way, Barbara Brown Taylor addresses the same transition in *Leaving Church* (2006). If you are hanging on by a thread, I encourage you to read one or both of these.

First, what about religion? I write as a Christian with most of my knowledge having to do with North American Christianity. My first response to the question, however, is larger than Christianity. The first thing I want you to know is that a lot of religion today has been hijacked by fundamentalism. Christianity has been as well.[12] While this is a complex matter, it essentially means that legalism has replaced love, judgmentalism has replaced oneness, and retribution has replaced restoration. Grace has diminished and a perfectionistic works-righteousness has increased.[13] Mix this into the growth of dualistic thinking (either/or, in/out, and right/wrong) and you have the makings of toxic religion and deformative Christianity. So, the first thing I want to say is that you may have rejected a counterfeit spirituality (even though it may have been represented as orthodox and true) and, if that is the case, you have done a good thing by rejecting it. I am amazed at how many folks are able to sniff out the noxious odors better than those who inhabit a religious or ecclesial environment. If you are one of them, good for you!

Walking away, however, is not the answer. You may have escaped the fire, but that still leaves you homeless. Destruction is never sufficient. There must be new construction.[14] One way that new construction begins is by recalling that one meaning of the word *religion* is to keep things from falling apart. It's the image of

---

12. Paul W. Chilcote, *Active Faith* (Abingdon Press, 2019). In this book, my good friend looks at four things that are weakening or undermining Christianity in our day; fundamentalism is one of them.

13. Philip Yancey wrote perceptively about the loss of grace in *Vanishing Grace* (Zondervan, 2018).

14. I recommend some of the videos by Stan Mitchell, available online at EverybodyChurch.com. Stan went through the deconstruction and then new construction experience in his own life, and did so as the pastoral leader of a church in Tennessee. His insights into the process are on-target, valuable, and encouraging.

the metal bands that encircle a barrel to keep it from collapsing. Another meaning of religion is to restore something that's been hurt or lost by giving attention to it, caring about it, and healing it.[15] Simply put, true religion is about restoration and renewal; it's about a renovative experience that takes place in the atmosphere of grace and the practice of love.

Making religion an attractive element in life occurs for many people today through an embrace of what is often called the perennial tradition, that is, the primary elements of religion before there were particular religions. Here again, some people find that what they gave up on was not religion, but the execution of organized religions that exist to represent it. They come to see that they have given up on the containers, while remaining deeply interested in the content. The perennial tradition emphasizes these things: (1) there is one Divine Reality inherent in, and around, everyone and everything; (2) the Divine Reality is mystery—that is, it can never be fully described but it can be noted and pointed to; (3) all creation longs to be consciously "in" Divine Reality, not settling for a generic existence with it (as all things are) but a life-giving expression of it; and (4) the final goal of all existence is union with Divine Reality.[16]

I am willing to guess that all four of these things remain alive in you, no matter how you have experienced the world's religions. I would wager that you would be interested in a community

15. Michael Mayne, *Giving Attention: Becoming What You Truly Are* (Canterbury Press, 2018), 2.

16. To explore the perennial tradition in more detail, I recommend these books: (1) Aldous Huxley, *The Perennial Tradition* (Chatto & Windus, 1969); (2) Bede Griffiths, *Universal Wisdom* (HarperCollins, 1994); (3) Houston Smith, chapter nine in *The World's Religions* (HarperCollins, 1991); (4) Richard Rohr, *A Spring Within Us* (CAC Publications, 2016); and (5) Karen Armstrong, *The Great Transformation* (Alfred Knof/Random House, 2006).

where these things could be cultivated in your life. In other words, I don't think you have actually walked away from religion (the content), but rather have walked away from religions (the containers). In fact, I don't think we can walk away from religion because we are made in the image of God and, as such, we have an insatiable hunger for God.

That leads to the second question: What about the church? The "Nones and Dones" I know best are those related to the Christian faith. Like many other religions, however, too much of Christianity has been overtaken by a fundamentalist and nationalist mindset. Some escapees have coined the term *churchless Christianity* to describe the origin of their exodus. I understand the sentiment of the term, but I don't believe it describes the substance what is really going on. For when the church is understood at its highest and best, it is impossible to be "churchless."

The church as we describe it in this book is not synonymous with the word *church* when used to describe an institutionalized expression of Christianity. The church is the body of Christ. When we remember this, it is impossible to imagine having life in Christ without being in Christ's body. But as with the word *religion*, the word *church* needs to be returned to its true meaning. The first step toward this recovery is admitting that when Jesus talked about building his church (Matt 16:18), he did not mean the institutionalized church.[17] In fact, I am persuaded that if he entered many of the churches today, the first thing he would do is what he did when he entered the temple: overturn the tables and

---

17. I believe this holds true for the other uses of the word *church* in the New Testament. To look at churches today and believe the first churches were like ours is a mistake. In fact, it can be argued that the churches as we see them in North America today have come to look as they do largely in the twentieth century, with some expressions (e.g., the mega church) emerging in the last thirty years or so.

drive out the money changer! He would exclaim today, as he did then, "*My house will be called a house of prayer. But you've made it a hideout for crooks*" (Matt 21:13). I realize this is a harsh thing to say, but I am among those who believe that it is time to be starkly honest about a lot that's going on in the church today that is unrepresentative of Christ and unworthy of Christianity. As you read this, don't forget that I say this as one who has given sixty years of my life in service to Christ through the church. Harsh though it may be, it is a lover's quarrel.

This quarrel demands reconnecting with the essence of the church. The word for it is *ecclesia*, and it is a word generally used to describe an assembly of people. When applied to the gathering of Jews and later Christians, it meant an assembly called together by God for the purpose of listening to God and being active for God. For Christians, it is an assembly where the risen Christ is the head, and where the gathered ones affirm his lordship over their lives. In our embrace of Christ's lordship, the church moves beyond being an assembly to being a metaphorical expression of Christ's body—a continuation of his life and work in the world, through the inspiration of the Holy Spirit. As such, the church has no official building, but what it does have is life together in Jesus's name.[18] The church is the gathering that incarnates the reality Jesus himself described as, "where two or three are gathered in my name, I'm there with them" (Matt 18:20).

This view of the church does not force us to choose between the invisible and visible expressions of church. It is entirely possible to find the invisible church in the visible (physical) churches, and many do so. It is possible to find the formative environment

---

18. My summary of the meaning of *church* is adapted from William Barclay's description of it in *New Testament Words* (SCM Press, 1964), 68–72.

we have looked at in this chapter in the churches, and many do so. However, it is also possible to find that environment outside institutional Christianity, and there are times when that is where we must look to find it. In other words, the recovery of church is not the abandonment of it, but rather the distinction between it and the institutional expressions we find of it—which may or may not be healthy expressions.

If you are in a quandary about the church, I understand. The church does not have one expression today. We have no choice but to discern the real from the less-real. What we do with the church will likely include struggling with the relationship between our desire to be in the body of Christ and the tangible place where that desire can be formed in a good way. We have no choice today but to seek God's wine while being more careful with respect to the wineskin from which we drink. This means holding the invisible church and its visible (physical) churches in a tension that sometimes allow them to coexist and, at other times, not. The main thing is not to allow deformative churches to rob you of the invisible church. What Jesus had in mind for the invisible church preceded the many visible churches and is different from them. Keep the two together, wherever and however you can, but never equate the wineskin with the wine.[19]

The concluding (but not final) word about the environment where life in Christ is formed is this: the environment exists. It is

---

19. In writing about differentiating between churches and the church, I realize I have left a lot unsaid. In fact, conditions vary so widely that I am not sure there is one "final word" to be spoken about the topic. One outstanding question has to do with the sacraments. For many of us, we must practice baptism and the Eucharist in an established congregation, but there is a growing number of other ways to experience both. We have not seen the culmination of these fresh expressions, so for the time being we have to "mix and match" the best we can, always keeping the kind of formative environment described in this chapter as our guiding light.

real. Seek for it and find it. With respect to the individual environment, make regular visits to your inner room (the cave of your heart) and commune in solitude and silence with God. As for the communal environment, gather regularly with others who are seeking to live in Christ. It may be inside the church, outside of it, or a mixture of the two—but in the words of Hebrews, "don't stop meeting together with other believers" (Heb 10:25). Life in Christ occurs where our individual environment intersects and interacts with the communal environment.

The Aim

Growing up in the 1960s as a teenager, the word *freedom* was important to me. Part of it had to do with the natural yearning for freedom that comes with being an adolescent, but a lot of it had to do with the decade in which I was living. I read Martin Luther King Jr.'s books, *Stride Toward Freedom* and *Strength to Love* as soon as I became aware of them.[1] The 1960s had barely begun before Dr. King was leading a movement that declared, "the time for freedom has come."[2]

Saint Paul said the same thing to the Galatians, "Christ has set us free for freedom" (5:1). Having been lured back to living in the flesh (legalism), their time for freedom (liberty) had come. This verse is the apex of Paul's letter, it is the verse toward which everything prior has been heading, and from which everything in the rest of the letter follows. As long as the Galatians lived by *sarx*,

---

1. Martin Luther King Jr., *Stride Toward Freedom* (Harper & Brothers, 1958) and *Strength to Love* (Harper & Row, 1963). I read King's other books as well, but these two made their initial and deep impact upon me.

2. Martin Luther King Jr., *I Have a Dream: Writings and Speeches that Changed the World*, ed. James M. Washington (HarperSanFrancisco, 1992), 73.

they would be in bondage; only by living in *pneuma* would they be free. Life in Christ is living in the Spirit.

My attraction to the idea of freedom in general, and as it relates to Paul's letter to the Galatians, has been heightened the past twenty years by Eugene Peterson's book, *Traveling Light: Modern Meditations on St. Paul's Letter of Freedom*.[3] Peterson describes his reason for choosing freedom as the interpretive lens for Paul's letter, "Since a free God is at the center of all existence, and all creation and every creature issues from a free act, freedom and not necessity is always the deeper and more lasting reality. At the center of that belief is Jesus, the freest person who ever lived."[4] I believe Paul would agree with Peterson's assertions: that freedom is the lasting reality, and that Jesus is the incarnation of that reality. Paul's desire for Christ to be formed in the Galatians individually and collectively was fueled by his vision for their freedom, a freedom that would be theirs because of Christ. Paul's aim for the Galatians is my aim in writing this book: to show that your life in Christ is one of freedom.

My problem in the 1960s was that the desire for freedom was met with a plethora of alleged ways to be so. The choices were confusing, and in relation to the Christian faith, some were contradictory. Our time is no different. Many freedom fantasies (the way Peterson puts it) exist today as they always have. In Paul's day, it was the faux freedom foisted on the Galatians by the Judaisers. On the level of the ego, living in the flesh made sense and had a strong attraction. That's why Paul refused to soft-peddle his sentiment, writing strongly, "You irrational Galatians! Who put a

---

3. Eugene Peterson, *Traveling Light: Modern Meditations on St. Paul's Letter of Freedom* (Helmers and Howard, 1988). Peterson uses the idea of freedom as the lens for reading and understanding Paul's letter to the Galatians.

4. Peterson, *Traveling Light*, 10.

spell on you?" (Gal 3:1). Again, Paul writes, "You were running well—who stopped you from obeying the truth? This line of reasoning [living in the flesh] doesn't come from the one who called you" (Gal 5:7-8).

The aim of life in Christ is freedom, but not just any kind of alleged freedom. The aim is freedom in Christ. But what does that mean? A response to that question begins to unfold when we understand that freedom is a twofold experience: freedom is a movement away from something and a movement toward something else. Paul's words capture the duality well: "Christ has set us free [from something] for freedom [to something]" (Gal 5:1). We understand our life in Christ by looking at it in both directions.

Christ has set us free **from** things. Within the context of Galatians, this is being set free from living in the flesh—from living egotistically and ethnocentrically. Christ has set us free from the false self and from the herd, both of which we have looked at previously in this book. In this sense, we can exclaim, "Free at last, free at last, thank God almighty, free at last!" In the broad sense, this is what Paul described as being set free from the law of sin and death (Rom 8:2). The theological word for this is *redemption*, a word that means being bought back from an illegitimate owner. Paul would have said to the Galatians, "You were never meant to live in the flesh"; he would say the same to us.

The Lord's Prayer enables us to consider what redemption looks like. When we pray the Lord's Prayer we say, "Don't lead us into temptation, but rescue us from the evil one" (Matt 6:13). The first phrase has confused many people, for it seems to say that God might lead us into temptation, and that doesn't square with what we know of God's nature. The fact is, however, the phrase does not say that, and the language tells us so: "do not lead us into" is one way (perhaps not the best way) of saying, "Lead us *away from*," for if we are not being led to something, then we are being led away from it. So we pray, "Lead us away from temptation," which is our way of telling God that we don't want to live under temptation's influence. This is the first part of our freedom: not falling prey repeatedly to temptation.

The second phrase, "rescue us from the evil one," goes deeper into the matter. It describes a life already under evil's influence, indeed a life already captive to evil. The Lord's Prayer offers us a great assurance, not only that can God give us the strength to withstand temptation, but also that God can rescue us when we are in temptation's grip. Both of these ideas are present in the first part of Galatians 5:1: "Christ has set us free." Whether it's the Lord's Prayer or this verse in Galatians, it is the Bible's way of saying that God has the last word—not temptation, not evil, not anything.

I have lived long enough to recognize areas in my life where I have been set free **from** things—some things in advance, and other things after I had fallen into their sway. I have also lived long enough to have met people who have been remarkably set free. All I can do at this point in the book is to ask you to consider your life: What have you been spared from, either before you fell prey to them, or afterward? For the Galatians it was Christ's deliverance from living in the flesh, which according to Paul's letter, essentially means freedom from the false self, freedom from legalism, and freedom from toxic religion. For us, it can be anything. It is what we mean when we sing, "Grace Greater Than Our Sin." Paul's aim in his letter is to bring the Galatians to the place of celebration, to the place of thanksgiving, to the place of gratitude; however, it goes on further from there.

Christ has set us free **for** things. It is not enough to be delivered from something; we must be directed into something else. Otherwise, we are in limbo, in a dangerous vacuum. Jesus spoke of this in the Parable of the Empty House, which is about a person whose spiritual house was cleansed of evil but was left empty (Matt 12:43-45). Because the house was left in that empty state, the evil spirit returned and brought seven other spirits along. The end result is that the "person is worse off than at the beginning" (12:45). The formative process includes an emptying (an abandonment, a surrender), but as good as that is, it is not enough. There must also be a filling (a receptivity, a consecration), and as we read through Paul's letter to the Galatians, we can see this second dimension of freedom coming into play. Nowhere is this clearer than in Paul's exhortation for the Galatians to produce the fruit of the Spirit in their lives (Gal 5:22-23). This is so important that we will focus on this aspect of life in Christ in the next chapter. For now, the fruit of the Spirit serves to remind us that our freedom in Christ is **for** a purpose. In broad categories, I see this second dimension of freedom in several significant expressions.

First, we are set free for the purpose of being human.[5] Have you ever thought to yourself or heard someone say, "Don't blame me, I'm only human!" We understand the sentiment of the exclamation, but the substance is dead wrong. Our fundamental problem is not that we are human; our dilemma is that we are not human enough. We have slipped beneath God's intention for us, which is to live as people made in God's image. It is striking that Paul described Jesus as "the image of God" and "the image of the invisible God" (2 Cor 4:4 and Col 1:15). We have already noted this, but it comes up again here. Jesus is the human one, the

---

5.   Jean Vanier, *Becoming Human* (Paulist Press, 1998).

walking, talking example of who we are meant to be in our humanity. With respect to freedom, Jesus is not only the example of our humanity but also he is the emancipator who makes us free.

This leads us directly to the second outcome of our freedom: we are free for the purpose of loving. Paul wrote eloquently about this in 1 Corinthians 13, leading us to the place of knowing that, of all the attributes of life, "the greatest of these is love" (13:13). We are never more like Christ—more like God—more like we were meant to be than when we love. Both the law and the prophets, Jesus said, hang on love: the love of God and loving others as we love ourselves (Matt 22:34-40). Martin Luther King Jr. understood freedom precisely this way by saying that through Christ we are given strength to love.

Here we must emphasize that, just as we are not talking about freedom as simply any kind of freedom, neither are we talking about love as simply any kind of love. Rather, we are talking about a kind of love rooted in God's nature and given to us by God, a love that both enriches us and moves naturally (as does God's love) through us to enrich others. Eugene Peterson noted that this is the only kind of love that can properly be linked with freedom: "Apart from love, freedom quickly disintegrates into the anarchy of the book of Judges when 'every man did what was right in his own eyes' [Judges 21:25]."[6] Love that stops with self-improvement is not God's kind of love. Freedom that ceases when we ourselves are free is not God's kind of freedom. Rather, as Jesus said, "Much will be demanded from everyone who has been given much" (Luke 12:48).

Finally, our freedom is for the purpose of service. Freedom is missional. This will be our focus in the next chapter. Again,

6. Peterson, *Traveling Light*, 152

Peterson says it clearly, "Freedom is not self-sufficiency but a shared life. The ideal is not independence, but interdependence."[7] E. Stanley Jones noted that one of the primary results of the atonement is that we're delivered from self-centered preoccupation (2 Cor 5:15).[8] This is at the heart of the second great commandment: "*You must love your neighbor as yourself*" (Matt 22:39). The words *as yourself* are not about us loving others the way we love ourselves, but are about loving others as if they were ourselves— because they are! We are all together in the single web of life. We not only interact, we inter-are. When we see this, independence is no longer an option. Servanthood is the way into life.

Jesus made no bones about it: "the one who is greatest among you will be your servant" (Matt 23:11). In this sentence we see both the personhood and the performance of life in Christ. The word Jesus used to describe the personhood of the servant was *diakonos*. The idea was so important in the early Church that it became an office of ministry: the deacon. Before it was a ministerial office, however, it was a spiritual disposition. To be a servant is to be someone who recognizes a higher way of life than selfishness, and gives themselves to that way. The word *diakonos* spans the range of service from the menial to the sacrificial, with each person finding their respective place in that spectrum. The Wesleyan Covenant Prayer puts this commitment into words: "Christ has many services to be done." To be a servant is to occupy our place with commitment.

With respect to the servant's performance, William Barclay wrote that we find a clue in the word *leitourgia*, which we translate

7. Peterson, *Traveling Light*, 175.
8. E. Stanley Jones, *Growing Spiritually* (Pierce & Washabaugh, 1953), 19.

in English as *liturgy*.[9] We commonly identify this word with a form of worship and, in that respect, it is our reminder that worship is the central act of God's people. The word itself, however, has deeper and wider meaning than this. It is a word that describes the actions people take voluntarily on behalf of others. There are things that need to be done, and there are people who recognize this and offer themselves in ways that get them done. Frederick Buechner believes that we find our place of service where "your deep gladness and the world's deep hunger meet."[10] We never feel more truly ourselves than when we live at this intersection.

It is almost impossible to overstate the importance of being other-oriented as a key element of the freedom in our life in Christ. As I write this, however, I am deeply troubled by the self-centeredness (individualism and nationalism) of our world.[11] Its roots are in the original sin of Genesis 3 (egotism and ethnocentrism); its manifestations are seen in the rest of the Bible and in the pages of history. Its essence is a superiority that expresses itself through power, control, discrimination, and subjugation. Ayn Rand's influence has resurfaced in the minds of many today, including in political and religious leaders' minds. Here in the United States we are under the influence of Christian nationalism, one tenant of which is its allegation that Jesus did not come to serve the masses, but only the few (the few meaning the wealthy elite).[12] This is pure heresy, but it is the way many live. It is Ayn

9. William Barclay, *New Testament Words* (SCM Press, 1964), 176–78.

10. Frederick Buechner, *Wishful Thinking* (Harper & Row, 1973), 95.

11. Walter Brueggemann writes powerfully about this in part two of *Tenacious Solidarity* (Fortress Press, 2018).

12. Jeff Sharlet wrote two powerful books about the influence of Christian nationalism in the world today: *The Family* (HarperPerennial, 2009) and *C-Street* (Back Bay Books, 2011). Ben Howe looks at the threat of Christian nationalism in *The Immoral Majority* (Broadside Books, 2019).

Rand's philosophy made to look like Jesus's message. Part of our call to freedom today is the challenge to engage in a prophetic ministry that challenges this fallen-world way of thinking and acting. I will return to this in the next chapter because the need to expose the lie of self-centeredness is so acute today.

Our freedom is the freedom to give what we have received. The old time, talent, and treasure trilogy summarizes the concept well, but each of these words opens up to a wider range of actions. There is no one-size-fits-all enactment of these three words, but each of us must identify aspects within each word in which we can invest ourselves so that the Word can continue to be made flesh (see John 1:1). In this respect, freedom is our reminder that the incarnation was not a one-time event, but is an ongoing paradigm of God's will for each of us. Beyond being human, loving, and serving, Eugene Peterson wrote that Gospel freedom is full-orbed; it is a freedom for all people to live, curse, change, resist, explore, think, fail, receive, trust, stand, create, and die.[13]

With that, we come full circle. We began with Martin Luther King Jr., and we end with him. As a teenager in the 1960s, I was moved by King's "I Have a Dream" speech in front of the Lincoln Memorial on August 28, 1963. The freedom he had spoken about, written about, and marched for since 1955 came together in his words that day. He called it a dream, but by the very way he delivered his message, it was more than that. It was a magnificent vision—a vision of a way of life that would bring freedom to all. I remember wanting that kind of freedom for myself, that very day and also wanting it for others. King's words

13. Peterson, *Traveling Light*. These are the chapter titles of his book and are his way of unpacking Paul's message in his letter to the Galatians.

still move me, and I cannot watch a film of that speech without those original feelings welling up inside of me again. It is the freedom I still yearn for—a freedom yet to be fully realized and a freedom from something into something else. It is a freedom not merely to name but also to enact. It is the aim of life. It is the aim of the Gospel. "Christ has set us free for freedom" (Gal 5:1). This is life in Christ.

Chapter Nine

The Mission

For my thirteenth birthday, my dad gave me his copy of the book he said had influenced his life more than any other, except for the Bible: Edgar A. Guest's *You Can't Live Your Own Life*.[1] The title says it all; namely, Guest's conviction is that our lives are not ours to live. He believed deeply that we live as we are meant to live when we live for the sake of others. This is a paradox, that we live most when we live beyond ourselves, but it is also a life-giving paradox.

Paul shared this view. After spending quite a bit of time in his letter to the Galatians about their need to move from living in the flesh to living in the Spirit, he wrote, "So then, let's work for the good of all whenever we have an opportunity" (Gal 6:10). The freedom we explored in the last chapter is a liberation that moves us beyond the imprisonment of self-centeredness into the emancipation of being other-oriented. E. Stanley Jones emphasized egocentrism and ethnocentrism as the first enemy of abundant

---

1. Edgar A. Guest, *You Can't Live Your Own Life* (Reilly & Lee Company, 1928). Guest was well-known in his day, largely for his writing at the Detroit Free Press and particularly for his poetry. He was also well-known because of his radio and television presence.

113

living after we cease to make God central. He wrote, "Every self-centered person is a self-disrupted person, even though he centers upon himself for religious motives."[2] Jones's description here connects directly with Paul's perspective, namely that even Paul's intense desire for the Galatians to have Christ formed in them would only reach its purpose if they lived beyond themselves for the good of all (4:19).

Life in Christ is missional. Jesus himself taught this in the Great Commission (Matt 28:16-20) and in his final words to his disciples before ascending to heaven (Acts 1:8). His own incarnation was the ultimate expression of God being other-oriented, which is the orientation of love (John 3:16). Paul summed this idea up well when he wrote that "we don't live for ourselves" (Rom 14:7). This has been the witness of Christianity for two thousand years. There is no abundant life (personally) and no life together (communally) unless there is life lived on behalf of others.[3]

When we hear that life in Christ is missional, we can easily shift our thinking toward activity, but activity is not where mission begins. Prior to practice, living missionally is an inward reality. At its deepest level, living missionally is living maturely, and E. Stanley Jones said it simply, "Maturity is outgoingness."[4] Conversely, immaturity is living with an absent or diminished inclination or capacity for involvement in others' lives. All the way back into the early history of Israel, God emphasized love for others,

---

2. E. Stanley Jones, *Abundant Living* (Whitmore and Stone, 1942), 43. Jones writes about the dangers of self-centeredness in Week 7 of this book, and it comes up throughout his many other books.

3. Dietrich Bonhoeffer wrote persuasively about this in chapter two of *Life Together* (Harper & Row, 1954).

4. E. Stanley Jones, *Christian Maturity* (Abingdon Press, 1957), 71.

which was a trait that was missing in other cultures and countries. Sadly, it is also missing in our world today.

"You must love your neighbor as yourself; I am the LORD" was the divine mandate; it was also the only verse Jesus quoted from the holiness code and then later referred to it as the second great commandment (Lev 19:18). The phrase "I am the LORD" is the defining element. The primary characteristic of Yahweh is love (*hesed* and *agape*), a love that, as we have already seen, manifests itself in mercy, faithfulness, forgiveness, and compassion. Life in Christ is missional in that it arises from the core of maturity, which is love.

Living missionally is also living *eucharistically*; it is living with gratitude.[5] Henri Nouwen used the sacrament of Holy Communion to describe living as those who have been taken (chosen), blessed, broken, and given.[6] With respect to the idea of givenness he wrote, "Our humanity comes to full bloom in giving."[7] In *With Burning Hearts*, Nouwen connected the idea of givenness to mission, drawing upon the two travelers' encountering Jesus on the road to Emmaus and being told, "Go and tell." About this commission, Nouwen writes, "Communion is not the end. . . . What you have heard and seen is not just for yourself. It is for the brothers and sisters and for all who are ready to receive it."[8]

With maturity and gratitude in place, we can now consider some ways God calls us to live missionally today. Needless to say,

---

5. David Steindl-Rast has been my main mentor with respect to gratitude. His book, *Gratefulness: The Heart of Prayer* (Paulist Press, 1984) is my mainstay. For a broader view of him and his views, however, I recommend the book edited by Clare Hallward, *David Steindl-Rast: Essential Writings* (Orbis Books, 2010). Diana Butler Bass has also written an excellent book, *Grateful* (HarperOne, 2018).

6. Henri Nouwen, *Life of the Beloved* (Crossroad, 1992).

7. Nouwen, *Life of the Beloved*, 85.

8. Henri Nouwen, *With Burning Hearts* (Orbis Books, 1994), 81.

there is a myriad of ways, but I believe they congeal in several fundamental and much-needed practices. These practices transcend Christianity, but they are seen in Christ's life and those who follow him. I begin with the practice of compassion. At least nine times in the gospels, Jesus encountered people in need and had compassion on them (e.g., Matt 9:36, 14:14). Compassion includes sympathy and empathy, but it also goes deeper than both. Compassion is being moved at the core of one's being by someone or something, and then being moved to action.[9]

The teachings of the Dalai Lama have helped me see the larger dimensions of compassion.[10] No matter where the Dalai Lama goes, he emphasizes kindness and compassion, not only observing their absence but more importantly, calling upon all humanity to embrace and express kindness and compassion in all our words and deeds. Along with many others, the Dalai Lama recognizes that compassion is evidence of maturity and (from his Buddhist vantage point) a mark of intelligence. Compassion is the sign that we have "a good heart." In fact, the idea of having a good heart is what the Dalai Lama believes the Buddha and Jesus agree on the most.[11] He observes the closeness in Jesus's teachings about loving our enemies, the sermon on the Mount (especially the Beatitudes), and God's kingdom. Similarly, Thich Nhat Hanh observes the Buddha/Jesus connection in, *Living Buddha, Living Christ*.[12]

---

9. William D. Mounce, *Complete Expository Dictionary of Old and New Testament Words* (Zondervan, 2006), 128–29.

10. Mary Craig, ed., *The Pocket Dalai Lama* (Shambala, 2002) is an excellent compilation of his writings that focus on compassion—its need in the world today, a need that, when expressed, is revolutionary.

11. Dalai Lama, *The Good Heart: A Buddhist Perspective on the Teachings of Jesus* (Wisdom Publications, 1996).

12. Thich Nhat Hanh, *Living Buddha, Living Christ*, 10th anniversary ed. (Riverhead Books, 2007).

I mention the Dalai Lama and Thich Nhat Hanh particularly because they both lived through intense persecution and demonstrated missional leadership over a long period.

Some of you may wonder why I bring non-Christian writings into my account of life in Christ. My answer is simple, although not everyone agrees with me. I understand Christ as the name Christians give to the primal source of existence.[13] John called this same concept *logos* (drawing upon classical Greek philosophy), saying that in Jesus "the Word became flesh" (John 1:14). Jesus did not hesitate to say, "I am the light of the world" (John 8:12). If Jesus understood himself in a way that was larger than his own time, place, and religion, then so can we. In fact, to view Christ as universal does not diminish who I believe him to be within Christianity; it increases what I believe.

Moreover, I believe that the missional aspect of our life in Christ inevitably brings us into communion and communication with non-Christians. All people yearn for Life (with a capital "L"), and every religion teaches its understanding of this Life, offering guidance into the experience of such a Life. Thomas Merton helped me see this through his own experience, which he described in this way: "I think we have now reached a stage of (long overdue) religious maturity at which it may be possible for someone to remain perfectly faithful to a Christian and Western monastic commitment, and yet to learn in depth from, say, a Buddhist or Hindu discipline and experience."[14]

Looking at life in Christ this way is not merely for our edification, it is also for our engagement in the pressing needs and

---

13. Richard Rohr, *The Universal Christ* (Convergent Books, 2019), 13.
14. Christine Bochen, ed., *Thomas Merton: Essential Writings* (Orbis Books, 2000), 174–75.

formidable challenges of our time. These things are beyond the scope of any person, group, or religion. Life in Christ calls us into life together with everyone else on the planet, journeying toward the common good. Because this takes place differently in different peoples, locations, and cultures, we are beckoned to take our faith in one hand (as our affirmation) and put our other hand into the hands of those around us (as our association), so that the will of God may be done on earth as it is in heaven.

What kind of person does this vision of life in Christ produce? A full answer to that question is beyond my expertise and beyond the scope of this book. I do believe, however, that it is summarized in Paul's phrase, "speaking the truth with love" (Eph 4:15). Esther de Wall wrote that this is an all-embracing love; Glenn Hinson called it living as horizontal persons.[15] It is maintaining our spiritual or religious home address while moving to the frontiers of life and the world. It is, as Thomas Merton put it, to be an explorer—a person who is "bound to search the existential depths of faith in its silences, its ambiguities, where there are no easy answers and where the division between believer and unbeliever ceases to be crystal clear."[16]

When I bring all of this back to Paul's letter to the Galatians, I see Paul describing this kind of life in Christ through the fruit of the Spirit (Gal 5:22-23).[17] The metaphor of fruit carries the idea of life, both with respect to its immediate lifegiving potential, and also because it contains the seeds from which additional

---

15. Both of these persons write respective essays about these two things in John Mogabgab's book, *Communion, Community, and Commonweal* (Upper Room Books, 1995), 175–87.

16. Bochen, *Thomas Merton: Essential Writings*, 46.

17. I remind you that E. Stanley Jones devoted twelve weeks (Weeks 18 through 29) of daily readings about the fruit of the Spirit in his book, *Growing Spiritually* (Pierce & Washabaugh, 1953).

life emerges. In this sense, the fruit of the Spirit is linked to life (*zoe*), which is what Jesus said he came to give. Theologically, it is important to notice that this is the fruit **of the Spirit**; it is the life of God dwelling in us and working through us. The fruit of the Spirit simultaneously describes our inner and outer life in Christ. The fruit of the Spirit shapes our character and directs our conduct.

We begin with love, which is the definition of life in Christ. I agree with John Wesley that love is "the root of all the rest."[18] Love is the sign that God's spirit dwells within us and is evidence that we abide in Christ (John 15:4). Love is the nexus of the two great commandments. Inwardly, we love God and outwardly we love others. *Love* is the first word Paul used to describe the fruit of the Spirit; as such, he is pulling together everything that has been said in scripture about *agape*, including all that he said in his other letters. The word *love* becomes a gathering of many insights into one laser beam that ignites our life in Christ.[19]

Next, we move to joy, the celebration of life. E. Stanley Jones put it simply: if Christ lives in us, we should notify our face![20] My friend and mentor, David McKenna, always signs his letters and emails "With His Joy" because he knows that joy is love celebrating, and his life exudes that joy. The manifestation of joy flows from a deep well of gratitude for our creation, redemption, and

18. See John Wesley, *Explanatory Notes Upon the New Testament* (1755) and his comment on Galatians 5:22. This may account for why Paul used the singular verb *is*, while going on to name eight additional characteristics. Whatever Paul's reason, however, there is a singularity to all nine words—a singularity that exists in love.

19. I remind you that E. Stanley Jones devote a year's worth of devotional readings to the subject of love in his book, *Christian Maturity*. Richard Rohr wrote two excellent books about love: *Eager to Love* (Franciscan Media, 2014) and *Richard Rohr: Essential Teachings on Love*, ed. Joelle Chase and Judy Traeger (Orbis Books, 2018).

20. Jones, *Growing Spirituality*, 139 (Week 20, Friday).

sustenance—all via the Spirit. In this sense, our joy is inevitable. However, it is also a quality of life that can be present in us regardless of our circumstances, simply because the basis of our joy is Emmanuel: God with us.

Paul's third word is peace, the wellness of life in Christ. Here Paul mines the meaning of the Hebrew word *shalom*, which means the comprehensive wellbeing that provides the strength, security, and stamina we need for long-haul discipleship. Peace includes being calm, but it is a calm borne of confidence that nothing can separate us from the love of God in Christ Jesus (Rom 8:38-39). This is confidence in God that goes all the way to the center of our lives. It is peace through and through. From that place, we become the peacemakers Jesus spoke about in the Beatitudes (Matt 5:9).

Because of such peace, we become patient. We have moved away from the edge of insecurity and the edginess of temperament. Because of the Spirit's work within us, we have been filled with the very patience toward others that God has toward us (Rom 15:5). The older word *longsuffering* is a good word, and it means we can endure people and things, even when (truth be told) we have every right to give up on them. James Moffatt called it being of "good temper" in his translation of the New Testament (Gal 5:22; Col 3:12).[21] This kind of patience is not apathy; rather, it means to hang in there because we genuinely believe change for the better is possible. For some, the very fact we are willing to stay with them is enough to bring them into that change.

No wonder, then, Paul could speak of kindness. In one way, this word sums up the rest of the fruits of the Spirit. As E. Stanley

---

21. James Moffatt, *The Holy Bible Containing the Old and New Testaments, A New Translation* (Chicago: University of Chicago Press, 1922).

Jones writes, without kindness "there is no virtue in the other virtues."[22] Kindness saturates the words both before and after it. We can think of it this way: kindness is the package within which all the other fruits of the Spirit are wrapped. This is not surprising, for we all have had experiences we remember for the rest of our lives because they came to us in the garment of kindness. Embedded in this virtue (and the others too, for that matter) is the Golden Rule of treating others the way we want to be treated. Kindness has been a precious gift for us to receive; it is also a precious one to give.

The next word is goodness, which is also translated from the original Greek as *generosity*. The difference in translation is not borne of confusion, but of scholars deciding what part of this particular fruit to emphasize. I like to keep both *goodness* and *generosity* together because each word tells us something about this aspect of the spiritual life. Goodness is the overarching word pertaining to creation itself; it is mentioned seven times in the first creation story and points to God's character. To be good in this sense is to be filled with God's spirit and to be in sync with the universe's purpose. To describe this as generosity is to emphasize that goodness is not minimalist. To exercise goodness is not to order our lives by the least we can do, but by the most. This kind of goodness and generosity overflows, and is akin to what Jesus taught when saying if someone wants your shirt, give them your coat too (Matt 5:40). This is goodness overflowing. It characterizes those who live in Christ.

Paul then says that the person who lives like Christ will demonstrate faithfulness. This means practicing fidelity not only with respect to our commitment to God, but also with respect to being considered trustworthy by others. We often put it this way, "You can count on him," or "You can rely on her." These kinds of people live with no hidden agendas. They do not practice bait-and-switch behaviors. They do not set things up with quid-pro-quo conditions that permit them to walk away if others do not measure up. Faithfulness says, "I am here, and I will be here." It is what Jesus said shortly before he ascended into heaven: "I am with you every day, even to the end of this present age" (Matt 28:20).

Next in the list of fruits is gentleness. Translators wrestle with how to translate this word from its original language, as well, because the idea of *gentleness* has already come through in kindness, goodness, and generosity. The word, however, stands on its own because it has other qualities worth noting. To be gentle is to be inwardly teachable and outwardly considerate. Gentleness takes the thorns off a rose, enabling us to be gracious receivers and givers. Gentleness is being open to life and adaptable in life. Gentleness eliminates preconceived notions and allows life to unfold realistically. Even when life comes at us with force or unfairness, we receive it in the spirit of the Serenity Prayer, accepting the things we cannot change and changing the things we can. As the prayer says, this kind of gentleness is wisdom.

Finally, the life Paul says God has in mind for us culminates in self-control. This is not control *by* the self, but rather the control *of* the self. This final word in the list of the fruits keeps the Spirit prominent in our lives. E. Stanley Jones believed that the evidence of self-control was contentment.[23] I have wondered if self-control is also one of the ways Paul described *sabbath* (restfulness) in the spiritual life. I have wondered if it is akin to what Buddhists mean when they say that the enlightened life is free from craving, that

23. Jones, *Growing Spiritually*, 194 (Week 28, Thursday).

the self is under control. Simply put, the self is not in charge, which is exactly how Jesus described the first mark of the blessed life in the Beatitudes (Matt 5:3).

This is the nine-word summary of the Christian life. It is important to see that it is one life; it is a whole life; it is a full life. It is not a life divided into nine territories or expressions. This is one reason why translators see overlapping meaning among many of the words. Each fruit of the Spirit is interconnected and interdependent. In a very real sense, the fruit of the Spirit expresses the divine dance within the Holy Trinity. The life of God is not cut up into three pieces or divided into three persons (who each have one-third of the pie); it is a singular life in which all the dimensions move with purpose, order, and influence. The fruit is meant to be with us as we live in Christ. In fact, at some point it is meaningless to ask whether something we said or did was kind, generous, or faithful. It just WAS, and what it was is Christlike. That's all that matters, for Christlikeness is our mission.

Even this is not the end of the story, however. Life in Christ leads us into what John Mogabgab called *commonweal*. It is the right word for this part of the chapter, but it is not one we use frequently. Commonweal means that we live for the sake of others.[24] Life in Christ is expressed because we have God's heart beating within us—a heartbeat for the general welfare of everyone and everything. Mogabgab explains it as an "orientation to the injured world beyond the congregation."[25] Commonweal is living in the spirit of Jesus, who said, "I have come down from heaven not to do my will, but the will of him who sent me" (John 6:38). This is

---

24. "For the sake of others" is how Robert Mulholland described it in his book, *Invitation to a Journey* (InterVarsity Press, 1993).

25. Mogabgab, *Communion, Community, Commonweal*, 12.

the apex of missional living. It is the reason Christ became incarnate in Jesus, and it is the reason the Word continues to be made flesh in us.

The need for commonweal is enormous in our day. We are drowning in a sea of self-regard fueled by egotism, ethnocentrism, and the partisanship and social eugenics they spawn. There are so many ways to illustrate God's call to us today to live beyond ourselves for the sake of others. For the purposes of this book, I refer to only two: vocational living and prophetic spirituality.

Vocational living means looking at our lives and the ways we have prepared ourselves to live those vocations by our education, experience, and circumstances—and then consecrating ourselves and our work to God (Rom 12:1). Vocational living includes the work we do, but it is more; it is also the particular life we live in relation to a sense of God's call upon us. In this way, vocational living does not describe the faith expression of a few, but rather the way of life every human being is meant to exhibit every single day.

I was speaking about this one evening at a men's group in Orlando, Florida. After I had finished my presentation and we had discussed as a group, the leader dismissed the meeting. Everyone had headed home, and I was gathering my notes and making ready to leave. I noticed that one man had stayed behind. I assumed he was the designated person to turn out the lights and lock the doors, so I hastened to get out so I would not delay him. I noticed that he followed me out of the room, however, leaving the lights on and the door open. He had stayed behind for another reason.

He wasted no time letting me know what the reason was: "I have been a member of this church since I was confirmed at age twelve, and I have been an attorney in Orlando for nearly thirty years. But tonight was the first time I have consciously connected being a disciple of Christ with being a lawyer." The way he told me just this little bit about his life revealed how deeply moved he was.

He continued, "Tomorrow morning, I have two appointments. The first is with a couple going through a divorce. The second is with a person facing bankruptcy. Tomorrow, for the first time in my life, I will care for them as an attorney and a disciple." By this time, we had reached the parking lot. He thanked me for coming, and we each headed to our own car. I have not seen him since; but he got it! He made the connection! The word *commonweal* was never used, but it was the dimension of life into which he had entered.

This is the missional life each of us is called to live, combining our faith with our everyday, accustomed duties. This is the broad meaning of "the sacrificial life," which William Temple said seems like no sacrifice at all because "when the care for others amounts to love, there is no pain; there is no feeling of even of conscientiousness; there is, instead, only an intense delight."[26] This is the naturalness of the spiritual life we have already noted. In fact, naturalness is the evidence that the life of Christ is within us and working through us. Beware of any spirituality that has to be contrived, exaggerated, or made self-referent.

With vocational spirituality in place, we move on to a second manifestation of missional living that is sorely needed in our day: prophetic spirituality. Sadly, we are living in a time when fundamentalism and nationalism has infected both politics and religion. In the United States, we are under the deformative influence of

26.   William Temple, *Christus Veritas* (St. Martin's Press, 1962), 221.

Christian nationalism.[27] I believe the threat it poses is so great that I cannot imagine writing a book about life in Christ at this time in our history without calling for nonviolent resistance against it.

The revived Poor People's Campaign, which Martin Luther King Jr. began in 1968, is emerging as a leading group in the United States that calls for the rejection of Christian nationalism. The campaign has identified systemic racism, imposed poverty, the war economy, and ecological devastation as key areas to address, with numerous sub-topics as well (e.g., the unjust criminal justice system, LGBTQIA discrimination, gun safety).[28] Similarly, the Pace e Bene ministry is prophetically challenging the un-Christian status quo through nonviolent resistance.[29] Additionally, Walter Brueggemann provided an excellent theological basis for prophetic resistance to nationalism that has significantly influenced me and many others.[30] Finally, Paul Chilcote has written about the peril of nationalism in his book, *Active Faith*.[31]

Life in Christ, as it is must be lived in our time, demands that we move into the church and society to speak and act prophetically in Jesus's name. Jesus himself gave us the images for doing this: salt and light (Matt 5:13-16). Missional living requires initiative to penetrate a world made tasteless and dark by sin; missional living gives flavor and illumination to life. Prophetic ministry calls

27. This is not a book meant to go into detail about Christian nationalism, but is a list of several books that will provide more details: Jonathan Wilson-Hartgrove, *Reconstructing the Gospel: The End of Slaveholder Religion* (IVP Books, 2018); Jeff Sharlet, *The Family: The Secret Fundamentalism at the Heart of American Power* (Harper Perennial, 2009); and Ben Howe, *The Immoral Majority* (Broadside, 2019).

28. For more information about the Poor People's Campaign, go to www.poorpeoplescampaign.org.

29. For more about Pace e Bene go to www.paceebene.org.

30. Walter Brueggemann, *Tenacious Solidarity* (Fortress Press, 2018). Most of his other books (beginning with *The Prophetic Imagination* [Fortress Press, 2018]) address the need for prophetic ministry and its nature in our time.

31. Paul Chilcote, *Active Faith* (Abingdon Press, 2019).

out fallen-world imperialism, calls up a willingness to look at life differently (repentance), and calls forth a vision of abundant living (*shalom*) for all who choose to live in God's kingdom. We have the opportunity to be instruments of God's peace in extending this witness in the world.

Obviously, there are ways to express missional living in addition to vocational and prophetic ministry. Hopefully, by referring to these two you have connected your desire for life in Christ with specific things you can do. In the Wesleyan Covenant Prayer, we find the words, "Christ has many services to be done." It's true! And whatever your specific ministry is, it will be one that enables you to foster "the practice of the better" as Richard Rohr writes.[32] It is what some today are calling the work to create a regenerative culture that increases life rather than depletes it. Buckminster Fuller speaks of Jesus's sentiment when he writes, "You never change things by fighting against the existing reality. To change something, build a new model that makes the old model obsolete."[33] I hope *Life in Christ* has been that kind of incentive for you.

Missional living is God's overarching call upon our lives to move beyond ourselves for the good of others. This is the communion, community, and commonweal movement we have been exploring. It is the divine flow of life. Parker Palmer described it thus: "The spiritual life, the inward life, the life of prayer faithfully pursued, will bring us back and back again to the public realm."[34] How could it be otherwise when we read that "God so loved the world" (John 3:16)?

32. Richard Rohr, "The Eight Core Principles" (Franciscan Media, 2013).

33. Ruth Gordon, "How Can We Shift to a Regenerative Culture in Every Sphere of Life?", Open Democracy, May 23, 2019, https://www.opendemocracy.net/en/transformation/how-can-we-shift-regenerative-culture-every-sphere-life/.

34. Parker Palmer, *The Company of Strangers: Christians and the Renewal of America's Public Life* (Crossroad, 1981).

Chapter Ten
The Culmination

I n the movie *City Slickers*, Mitch Robbins is in the midst of a midlife crisis, so he goes to a dude ranch to sort his life out. One evening, around the campfire, he asks Curly (the ranch's trail boss) to tell him the meaning of life.[1] Curly, a crusty old cowboy, raises one bony finger and says, "Just one thing, just one thing." He does not tell Mitch what that one thing is, but before the movie ends, we see that Mitch has found it. Mitch's question is one that we all ask sooner or later and in one form or another: "What is the meaning of life? What really matters? Where does it all end up?"

Paul ended his letter to the Galatians with the same questions on his mind, and he answered them simply: "What matters is a new creation" (Gal 6:15). Life in Christ is not static, nor is it on the move. It is not stationary; rather, it is headed somewhere. The spiritual life is a journey of culmination; it is an experience of abundant living in time and for eternity. As *Life in Christ* comes

---

1. *City Slickers* (directed by Ron Underwood, written by Lowell Ganz and Babaloo Mandel [Columbia Pictures]) was filmed in 1991 and stars Billy Crystal, who plays Mitch Robbins, and Jack Palance, who plays Curly.

to an end, the time is right to ask, "What is it all about?" Like Curly in *City Slickers*, I raise my bony finger and say, "One thing, just one thing." It's about new creation—a twofold reality that's about the here and now, and also about forever.

One of the problems with some versions of Christianity today is that salvation is interpreted as "going to heaven when you die." Salvation is a God-paved escape route to get us out of this present-evil age and into the land of eternal goodness.[2] Some have even called this divine fire insurance. However, this is not what Paul meant when he spoke of a new creation. In fact, it is not what Christians understood salvation to be until roughly the time of the Enlightenment. Folks who make salvation appear to be mostly other-worldly fail to mention that the idea is relatively new in Christian history.

In fact, Paul understood the new creation to begin here and now, not there and later. When Jesus said he had come to give us abundant life, he did not mean that it would kick in after we die (John 10:10). So, the first thing to say about life in Christ as a new creation is that it is life right now and right where we are. When Paul wrote about the new creation to the Corinthians and said it is an experience where "old things have gone away, and look, new things have arrived" (2 Cor 5:17), he meant it was life in the present moment, not one deferred to the future. He said it again a later in the same letter, "now is the day of salvation" (2 Cor 6:2).

This is so important if we are going to understand what life in Christ means, and what the experience of this life will be for us.

2. Marcus Borg writes about this in chapter one of *The Heart of Christianity: Rediscovering a Life of Faith* (HarperCollins, 2003).

Thomas Moore wrote about the necessity of a spirituality in the here and now:

> I feel so strongly about the value of finding spirit under the skin of ordinary ordeals that I am suspicious of spiritual writing that goes too plainly and directly to the higher atmospheres....In my view, spiritual writing need not always inspire and thrill. Its first task is to give our ordinary ordeals deep context and tools of transcendence. It should help us get through life rather than above or around it.[3]

I wholeheartedly agree, and I believe Jesus and Paul would too. The culmination of life in Christ is not something to be anticipated, it is something to be embraced. Of course, there are eternal dimensions, and we will turn to them later in this chapter, but not before we recognize the present-tense culmination Paul had in mind for the Galatians.

We see this in Paul making the effort to address the current problem among Galatian Christians. There is no sense of deferral in his writing, only a sense of immediacy. Living in the flesh must stop now. As we have already seen, he tells the Galatians that he will be in travail until Christ is formed, or re-formed, in them (Gal 4:19). The letter's tone is cast in the present tense so much so that Paul seems to be saying, "I expect to receive a response from you indicating that the problem has come to an end." This is the same tone we find in the rest of the Bible. The permissions and prohibitions are not meant to be enacted at some future time. We are meant to read the Bible and respond immediately.

There are other important indicators that one's current reality is where Paul grounded his understanding of new creation. Summing up much of what he had previously written, Paul said:

---

3. Philip Zaleski, ed., *The Best Spiritual Writing 2000* (HarperSanFrancisco, 2000), xxi-xxii, xxiii.

"If we live by the Spirit, let's follow the Spirit" (Gal 5:25). He does not mean at some future time or into heaven; rather, Paul intends a here-and-now application of the Gospel. The first ten verses of chapter six spell out some of the specifics of doing that: restoring anyone who does something wrong, carrying each other's burdens, avoiding foolish arrogance, being content with our own work and not comparing it with that of others, ensuring that teachers are duly compensated for their work, ceasing to live selfishly, and never tiring of doing good for the sake of all people. The new creation is not something deferred or exiting only in heaven; it is here now on earth.

Paul connects the new creation with Jesus's teaching about God's kingdom, which has an already-but-not-yet dynamic. Jesus began his ministry announcing that God's kingdom was at hand, that it was near and attainable, not far away and theoretical. Everything we have explored in *Life in Christ* has a present-tense applicability. In fact, when we are faithful to life in Christ here and now, then we move forward in our journeys, which eventually takes us to heaven. Abundant living is life in earthly time and for eternity.

Included in the present-tense realities of life in Christ is the reality of struggle. Paul writes about the passing away of the old and the coming of the new in only a few words, but between those two realities we experience challenges and difficulties. The old does not pass away quickly and easily; egotism and ethnocentrism do not abandon their thrones without a fight. Thomas Moore writes about this reality:

> some kind of spirituality arrives only after profound struggle and emotional entanglements, that perhaps rises like a clear sky after a dark and stormy rain. Rilke says that God has to be mined from

the earth as we stoop over in the underground shaft of our personal strivings and difficulties. Alchemists described the process as hefting a pickax and very slowly digging for the spirit in the lowlands of mountains and at the edge of flowing waters.[4]

I am grateful that a growing body of contemporary writing about the spiritual life reminds us that spirituality is never separated from reality and that, if we set out to live in Christ, we will meet with all sorts of obstacles along the way. Richard Rohr writes about this well, describing the transformative process as one of order, disorder, and reorder.[5] Rohr's phase of order roughly corresponds to Paul's notion of the "old" (the false), and Rohr's phase of reorder is akin to Paul's idea of the "new" (true self). Disorder is the phase in which our "private salvation project" (as Thomas Merton referred to it) must break down in some way, a way that Rohr calls necessary suffering.[6] Something in our current realty has to stop working; otherwise, we would never move beyond it. Something has to fail us or disappoint us. If nothing else, this experience is necessary to break us of the kind of arrogance Paul told the Galatians to abandon (5:26), so that we do not put our trust in "the system" (our internal ego or the external group) rather than in Christ.

Believe me, this is not negative; it is the essential letting go that Jesus described when he said we must deny ourselves and follow him (Matt 16:24). It is the essence of the freedom we looked at in chapter eight. We cannot examine the present-tense nature of the new creation without recognizing the inevitability of disorder. Rohr describes it this way: "It is *necessary in some form* if any

---

4. Zaleski, *The Best Spiritual Writing 2000*, xix.
5. Richard Rohr, *The Universal Christ* (Convergent Books, 2019), 243–48.
6. Richard Rohr, *A Spring Within Us* (CAC Publications, 2016), 119–30.

real life is to occur; but some of us find this stage so uncomfortable we try to flee back to our first created order—even if it is killing us."[7]

Unfortunately, we are living in a time when too many teachers of the spiritual life omit the disorder phase, leaving their followers to think that the only thing between the old passing away and the new coming is smooth sailing. Failing to include intermediate struggle, when people hit the rough waters of formation, causes them to think, mistakenly, that they don't have "the real thing." If they feel that way long enough, then they may abandon the whole enterprise, believing it was nothing more than a spiritual hoax. Ironically, it is the element of realism that keeps everything else alive. It is the note of realism that keeps the idea of the new creation in the present moment and not deferred to some future time. Life in Christ is not a "hot house" spirituality, but rather is one that exists in life as we are actually living it.

At the same time, however, it is more than what current reality can contain. God's kingdom has a not-yet dimension. The new creation is not fully realized here on earth; rather, time flows into eternity. For Christians, resurrection describes the movement from one sphere of existence to the other, that is, from earth to heaven. As wonderful as life in Christ is here on earth, we have not experienced it all. Paul described this in his first letter to the Corinthians: "*God has prepared things for those who love him that no eye has seen, or ear has heard, or that haven't crossed the minds of any human being*" (1 Cor 2:9). Here, Paul quotes Isaiah 64:4, showing that this vision of a new creation extending into eternity had been part of the Message for a long time. It must be part of the message of *Life in Christ* too.

7. Rohr, *The Universal Christ*, 245.

My wife, Jeannie, coined a phrase I want to use here to discuss the transition into the eternal dimensions of the new creation: "the mystery we call heaven." The older I get, the truer this phrase becomes. I want to be clear that in writing about heaven as the ultimate culmination of our lives in Christ, I am not even scratching the surface of what that culmination really is. If Paul wrote that heavenly things haven't even crossed the mind of any human being, then surely I am not presuming to offer you "breaking news" about eternity in this book! Heaven is mystery. Mystery, and the metaphors used to describe heaven (e.g., golden streets in a celestial city), are not literal depictions, but rather are writers' attempts to stretch language as far as it can go to describe heaven. The stretch itself does not tell us everything, but neither does it leave us in the dark. Here are some things we can say with confidence about life in Christ beyond the present.

First, it is real. Jesus nailed that down himself when he spoke of the Father's house, and said that if it were not so, he would not have spoken about it (John 14:2). This is one of the reasons why I give more attention to the universal Christ these days. Richard Rohr's book, *The Universal Christ*, is my reference point, but it has also catapulted me in many directions. Prior to that, E. Stanley Jones's description of the excarnate Christ (before and after the incarnate Christ, Jesus) set my theological and formational journey in this larger context. Aging has also played a constructive role. I have lived long enough to have known people who came to the end of their days on earth and experienced connections with heaven that cannot be denied. Heaven is mystery, but it is also real.

Second, life in Christ is better in heaven that it is on earth. E. Stanley Jones said it simply: if heaven is not better than what we have known here, then who would want to go there? John made no bones about it as he brought his revelation to an end, saying that in heaven there would be no more mourning, crying, pain, or death "for the former things have passed" (Rev 21:4). This is what Paul had in mind when he said that the "old" would pass away. The betterment of our lives in heaven is in relation to the nature of God, whose purpose is to make all things new.

Third, God has been, is, and will continue to be at work to bring these things to pass. Paul wrote to the Ephesians, saying, "God revealed his hidden design to us, which is according to his good will and the plan he intended to accomplish through his Son. This is what God planned for the climax of all times: to bring all things together in Christ, the things in heaven along with the things on earth" (Eph 1:9-10). He wrote similarly to the Colossians saying that God has "reconciled all things to himself through [Christ]—whether things on earth or in the heavens" (Col 1:20).

Some have shied away from these verses for fear of teaching universalism. I believe, however, we have done a great disservice to religion in general, and Christianity in particular, by avoiding them. It is not my purpose to address universalism here, however, it is my purpose to point out that in both passages, universality is described with the words *all things* and the phrase "heavens and earth." Universalism (i.e., who is saved and how they are saved) is a theological issue that equally sincere Christians disagree about.

But here is what is not up for grabs: the heart of God is bent toward universality. God's plan from the beginning points to universality, and God's redemption through Christ is set in the context of universality (Col 1:20). There is no doubt about this. We are in relationship with the God "who wants all people to be saved" (1 Tim 2:4). How that gets played out through the grace of God is part of the mystery. But there is no misunderstanding God's intent: it is universality. You cannot take yourself out of that picture. No one can! The culmination of life in Christ is in eternity.

Conclusion

I began this book thinking of Nicodemus and his visit with Jesus, imagining that in many ways we are like him in our desire to know what life is meant to be and what really matters. As this book comes to an end, I am thinking about Nicodemus again, only this time I am wishing it were possible to sit down with him for a visit and ask, "So, what was it like to have a conversation with Jesus?" I imagine talking with him would be as fascinating as the conversation was between him and Jesus, recorded for us in John 3.

I believe that E. Stanley Jones came close to describing what Nicodemus would have said. Jones believed that when anyone experienced the presence of the risen Christ in their life, they would exclaim, "For this I am made!" For one to recognize life as Christ made it (John 1:3) and as God intended it (Gen 1), would be to overcome every barrier erected against it, whether by accident, circumstance, or rebellion. This overcoming would be natural, for we would see that we have been invited to live the way God wants us to live, and the way we want to live. Abundant life is the life we long for. I bet Nicodemus felt this way also, and his experience was soon repeated by St. Paul as he wrote to the Galatians about life in Christ.

I hope this book has explored life in Christ in such a way that such a life is your heart's desire too. I imagine some of you may read *Life in Christ* prior to professing faith in Christ. I hope this book might move you to commit your life to him. Notice that I wrote *to him*, not *to a particular institutionalized expression of him*.[1] I also imagine that people who are already Christians may read *Life in Christ* and, if you are such a person, I hope that in reading it you will see life in Christ is a never-ending journey. Life in Christ is neither a destination nor an arrival; it is a quest. Discovering life in Christ is not the end of the story, it is the beginning of it. We can never exhaust the life God has in store for us. We can always take another step in faith.

I also imagine that some of those who read this book adhere to other religions. I hope *Life in Christ* helps you recognize the universal Christ's presence in your faith tradition and in your life. I really do believe in the cosmic Christ, and I believe the presence is pervasive, not just within the world's religions, but within every aspect of life, from the smallest particle to the farthest star. I believe that the loss of this comprehensive perspective has reduced the message of religion in general, and Christianity in particular. This reduction gives our egotism and our ethnocentrism ground to allege that our limited view is sufficient when it is not. I hope *Life in Christ* has rooted you deeply in Christ and simultaneously blown the sides off any boxes you have been put in by your own

1. I have already made it clear that I do not separate Christ from the church, but here is the time to say again that I do not equate life in Christ with being a member of any particular church. Life in Christ is a universal reality; membership in a church is a choice based on many options. I invite you to Christ and leave it to you to decide about the role of the church in your life.

thoughts or others' influence. I hope this book leaves you with a holy "Wow!" If you adhere to another religion, I hope *Life in Christ* enables you to see Christ in it, for he is there.[2]

When I was invited to write this book, the invitation included the hope that it would be useful both to clergy and to lay leaders in the church. If you happen to be such a person, I hope you will find this book useful in your ministry. The appendices are meant to further assist you in making *Life in Christ* a beneficial resource for a ministry of spiritual formation in your local church.

Coming to the end of this multi-faceted exploration of three words—*life in Christ*—leads me to ask myself: What does it all boil down to? What is life in Christ in a nutshell? I believe it is (as Jesus himself said it is) the two great commandments: loving God and loving others as yourself (Mark 12:31). Every day the news and media deliver repeated examples in which a lack of love has prevented God's will to be done on earth as it is in heaven. Some of these lacks are horrible and threaten our planet. Others are less so. But every single failure to love reduces life as God intends it to be. We have been made by Love, for love.

Our purpose for living is to be lovers. *Life in Christ* is simply the three-word summary of our call to love. Christ is the goal and the pattern for life. If I could reduce everything we have considered in this book down to one thing, it would be this: decide to be a student of love with the aim of becoming a person in love, using Christ as your pattern. The truth is, you already are a person of love because you are made in God's image. You are God's beloved, and you are an instrument of God's love, here and how. About all that's left to say is this, and I say it to myself as I write it to you: act like it!

2. Thich Nhat Hanh wrote a wonderful book showing the presence of Christ in his chosen religion of Buddhism: *Living Buddha, Living Christ*, 10th anniversary ed. (Riverhead Books, 2007).

Appendices

I n addition to reading *Life in Christ* for personal enrichment, this book is also intended to be a resource for small groups and a means to go beyond what you have read. The following appendices are included to help you do both:

Appendix One: use this suggested guide to foster personal reflection and group discussion about each chapter in the book.

Appendix Two: this material will help you develop a small-group meeting format, not only while you explore this book, but also for ongoing group formation.

Appendix Three: you have likely noticed that many references in this book are to E. Stanley Jones's writings. This is intentional. Use this appendix as a reading journey into exploring his books in more depth. Jones's books are not listed by publication date, but rather in a way that enables you to follow his developing thoughts.

Appendix Four: devotional classics enrich our spiritual formation. This list of brief and selected works is compiled chronologically.

Appendix Five: in addition to the classics in appendix four, this list provides additional noteworthy writings that can enrich your spiritual formation.

Appendix Six: this list is a reference of works and one-volume overviews of Christian spirituality to use in studying a host of topics and people related to the spiritual life.

Appendix Seven: this list of spiritual formation ministries will help you develop an ongoing ministry of spiritual formation in your local church.

Appendix One

You can use the following questions for personal meditation after reading a chapter. You can also use this list as a guide for small-group discussion.

1. What word, phrase, or idea stands out for you after reading the chapter?

2. Why do you believe this word, phrase, or idea is important for you right now?

3. How can you use the word, phrase, or idea for your personal enrichment?

4. How can you use the word, phrase or idea to benefit others?

When using these questions in a small-group setting, some people like to go through them one at a time, creating a fourfold cycle for each meeting. Others prefer to have each person engage with all four questions before moving to the next person. Choose the pattern that works best for your group.

Appendix Two

If you are already part of an ongoing small group, you may not need this guide. If you are launching a small group experience, however, you may find it helpful. If you do use it, keep things flexible and interactive. This is not a format to follow mechanically, but rather it is a format to encourage a flow that will hopefully help make your time together a means of grace. The suggested time frame is one hour, but you can adjust accordingly.

Gathering (ten minutes): welcome one another and engage in lighthearted conversation to get settled into the meeting.

Silence (five minutes): sit quietly together, getting centered and present in the moment; ask God to make you receptive to the experiences you are about to have.

Conversation (thirty minutes): using the guide in appendix one (or some other accustomed format), discuss your reading of the assigned chapter (or other segment) of the book.

Silence (five minutes): sit quietly together, prayerfully considering the main "God word" (i.e., the word, phrase, or idea from the group exercise in appendix one) that you received.

Intercessions (five minutes): let those who desire to do so share their prayer requests. When a person completes his or her request, let the group respond: "Lord in your mercy, hear our prayer."

Closing (five minutes): the session's leader reminds group members what the next reading assignment is, when the next group meeting is, and any other pertinent information.

Appendix Three

I have intentionally woven E. Stanley Jones's perspectives through *Life in Christ*. Jones's writings continue to speak a much-needed message to individual Christians and to the church. If you wish to allow him to speak further to you, use the following "path" to journey with Brother Stanley further into life in Christ:

The Way**
Abundant Living**
The Word Became Flesh
In Christ**
Growing Spiritually**
Christian Maturity

E. Stanley Jones has written other books, and you can read them as you like. The titles listed above are chosen to create a reading journey that further shapes your experience of life in Christ. All the titles are available, and those marked with two asterisks (**) are available as e-books. Abingdon Press has reprinted these and other books by Brother Stanley, with additional ones to come.

Appendix Four

The writer of Hebrews said that we have a "great cloud of witnesses surrounding us" as we live the Christian life (12:1). Many of these witnesses have written about the spiritual life, and we refer to their works as devotional classics. Any spiritual formation diet should include an ongoing reading of these historic writings. The following list, arranged by time periods, is a very brief and selective recommendation of these devotional classics.

Early Christianity (100–500)
The Didache
The Sayings of the Desert Fathers (and Mothers)
Gregory of Nyssa, *The Life of Moses*

The Middle Ages (500–1500)
The Rule of St. Benedict
Bernard of Clairvaux, *The Love of God*
Saint Francis of Assisi and Clare, Classics of Western
  Spirituality series
Julian of Norwich, *Revelations of Divine Love*
Catherine of Genoa, *Life and Teaching*
Thomas à Kempis, *The Imitation of Christ*
Teresa of Ávila, *The Interior Castle*

Reformation Period (1500–1800)

Francis de Sales, *Introduction to the Devout Life*

Brother Lawrence, *The Practice of the Presence of God*

Jean-Pierre de Caussade, *The Sacrament of the Present Moment*

John Bunyan, *Pilgrim's Progress*

Henry Scougal, *The Life of God in the Soul of Man*

John Wesley, *The Standard Sermons*

Post-Reformation to the Present

The Philokalia

Søren Kierkegaard, *Purity of Heart is to Will One Thing*

Evelyn Underhill, *The Spiritual Life*

William Temple, *Christian Faith and Life*

Thomas Kelly, *A Testament of Devotion*

Dietrich Bonhoeffer, *Life Together*

Howard Thurman, *Jesus and the Disinherited*

Dorothy Day, *The Long Loneliness*

Thomas Merton, *New Seeds of Contemplation*

Richard Foster, *Celebration of Discipline*

Henri Nouwen, *The Return of the Prodigal Son*

Appendix Five

The list of devotional classics in appendix four does not scratch the surface of other noteworthy writings. The following list of names (and one text that has an anonymous author) is intended to help you find other writers across the ages who can help enrich your life in Christ.

John Cassian
Saint Augustine
The Cloud of Unknowing
Saint John of the Cross
Catherine of Siena
John Woolman
William Law
George Fox
Madame Guyon
Ignatius of Loyola
Hannah Whitall Smith
C. S. Lewis
Black Elk
Douglas V. Steere
Frank Laubach
Elizabeth O'Connor
Sadhu Sundar Singh
Susan Muto
Marjorie Thompson
Jan Richardson

Oscar Romero
Eugene Peterson
Richard Rohr
Parker Palmer
Barbara Brown Taylor
Frederick Buechner
Dallas Willard
Rachel Held Evans
Martin Luther King Jr.

Appendix Six

In addition to classic and contemporary works and writers, there are a number of reference volumes that provide an array of entries about the spiritual life. The following are particularly helpful.

> Keith Beasley-Topliffe, *The Upper Room Dictionary of Christian Spiritual Formation*
>
> Evan Howard, *The Brazos Introduction to Christian Spirituality*
>
> Cheslyn Jones, et al., *The Study of Spirituality*
>
> Gordon Wakefield, *The Westminster Dictionary of Christian Spirituality*

There are also some notable one-volume overviews of Christian spirituality that provide a big-picture perspective.

> Lawrence Cunningham and Keith Egan, *Christian Spirituality: Themes from the Tradition*
>
> Urban T. Holmes, *A History of Christian Spirituality*
>
> Robin Maas and Gabriel O'Donnell, *Spiritual Traditions for the Contemporary Church*
>
> Bradley Nassif, et al., *Four Views on Christian Spirituality*
>
> Richard Woods, *Christian Spirituality: God's Presence Through the Ages*

Appendix Seven

We are fortunate to have a number of parachurch organizations devoted to resourcing ministries of spiritual formation in the local church. Each of these has a website that provides additional information and a host of resources.

The Apprentice Institute: led by James Bryan Smith, this ministry offers a variety of resources and programs for individuals and congregations.

Companions in Christ: this series of studies from The Upper Room is an excellent resource for exploring foundational aspects of the Christian spiritual life.

Renovaré: begun years ago by Richard Foster, and now in its second generation of leadership, this ministry is a full-service resource for individuals, groups, and congregations.

CPSIA information can be obtained
at www.ICGtesting.com
Printed in the USA
LVHW032106250720
661518LV00007B/10